MYTHS AND MYSTERIES SERIES

MYTHS AND MYSTERIES

OF

FLORIDA

TRUE STORIES
OF THE UNSOLVED AND UNEXPLAINED

E. LYNNE WRIGHT

Guilford, Connecticut

To my dad, who taught me to love learning, and my mom,
who taught me to love books.
And to the best family in the world: mine.

To buy books in quantity for corporate use
or incentives, call **(800) 962-0973**
or e-mail **premiums@GlobePequot.com**.

Map © Morris Book Publishing, LLC
Project editor: Meredith Dias
Layout: Maggie Peterson

Library of Congress Cataloging-in-Publication Data

Wright, E. Lynne, 1931-
  Myths and mysteries of Florida : true stories of the unsolved and unexplained / E. Lynne Wright.
      p. cm.
  Includes bibliographical references and index.
  ISBN 978-0-7627-6967-4
  1. Florida—History—Anecdotes. 2. Florida—Social life and customs—Anecdotes. 3. Curiosities and wonders—Florida—Anecdotes. 4. Florida—History, Local—Anecdotes. 5. Florida—Biography—Anecdotes. I. Title.
  F311.6.W76 2013
  975.9—dc23
                                        2012004541

Printed in the United States of America

10 9 8 7 6 5 4 3 2

CONTENTS

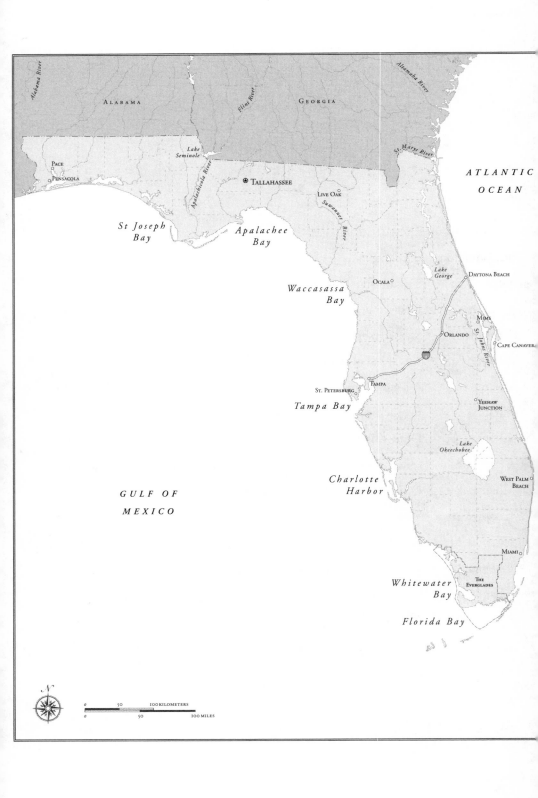

ACKNOWLEDGMENTS

For sharing their thoughts, photos, suggestions, and time, in conversations and by e-mail, I thank Fred Milch, John MacDougall, Larry E. Arnold, Bonnie Gross, Debi P. Wilkie, E. Gaines, Lan Nghiem-Phu, and Michael Pocock. Thanks to Tammy Evans for so generously sharing information she worked hard to uncover and for the outstanding and important book she wrote. I also want to thank the helpful staff at the Florida State Archives in Tallahassee, Margaret Perringer at the Kennedy Space Center, and Rhonda and Joe at the Desert Inn.

A thousand thanks to my outstanding editors, Erin Turner and Courtney Oppel, both always wise, patient, and a real pleasure to work with. Special thanks for so much technical help to George F. Wright, MD.

INTRODUCTION

In a state whose history stretches from long before the Pilgrims landed on Plymouth Rock to an era that sent men to walk on the moon, it should surprise no one that Florida's archives include more than a few mysteries. There have been so many years for strange happenings to occur in the dense forests, for mystifying encounters with red-skinned people, for eerie sounds to emanate from the dark jungles, for animals to appear that had never been seen before—and that was just the beginning.

Attracted by the climate, settlers ventured to the Land of Flowers from all over the world, as they still do. In the beginning, there were no Pilgrims named Calvin or Smith or Winthrop in Florida. Rather, people with names like Narváez and de Soto and Menéndez explored her jungles, prairies, and swamps. Instead of turkey and cranberries, Florida had grouper and oranges, more pelicans and egrets than robins and blue jays. Things are different here, future ads rightly proclaimed. But people are pretty much the same everywhere. We all need some amusement and occasional relaxation.

With no television, no computers, and no iPads, early Floridians told stories to each other for entertainment, many about the mysteries that surrounded them every day.

Speaking of being surrounded, with a coastline about 2,276 miles long, the state is nearly encircled by ocean, and what is more mysterious than whatever lies deep beneath it?

Someone said mysteries that last a long time beget myths, so it follows that the Sunshine State can also claim more than the usual number of myths. Florida tells stories of the Native Americans, the Spaniards, the English, and the people from every other part of the globe who came to live in this fabled land. Tales about people's homelands, origins, moral values, history, and religion have become myths. But in Florida, it didn't stop there. Now myths are told about Disney World and the astronauts.

Folklore has a way of bringing us together, explaining the mysteries of the world, passing on wisdom, or simply amusing us. It fills a need that television, computers, and iPads cannot. As the state more and more becomes a victim of its own enchantment, it is essential that we protect her vanishing magic by continuing to retell her myths and mysteries.

CHAPTER 1

The Elusive Florida Skunk Ape

What walks like a man, looks like an ape, and smells like a skunk? In the area north of the Everglades, that question stumps no one. The answer is the Florida Skunk Ape and, dear reader, be forewarned that you would most likely smell him long before you would see him.

Most certainly there are skeptics, but you may want to keep an open mind about it—particularly when nearly all Native American tribes have acknowledged belief in such a creature for hundreds of years, other Floridians have reported similar sightings for decades, the Florida Fish and Wildlife Conservation Commission operates a file on such sightings, and even respected scientists, although expressing doubt, still maintain the possibility of the creature's existence.

In the early fall of 2000, the Sarasota County Sheriff's Office received a letter from an anonymous woman containing two photographs of a creature she assumed was an escaped orangutan. The woman wanted to know if anyone had reported a missing orangutan. She said she was a senior citizen living with her husband near Interstate 75 and Myakka River State Park, and she explained how she came to have the photos of the animal.

"For two nights prior," she said, "it had been taking apples, which my daughter brought down from up north, off our back porch. These pictures were taken on the third night it had raided my apples. It only came back one night after that and took some apples that my husband had left out in order to get a better look at it." She thought the animal to be six-and-a-half to seven feet tall in a kneeling position. On the night she went outside to take the photos, she heard the creature making deep "whoomp" noises and smelled its "awful smell that lasted well after it had left my yard." She and her husband watched for it to return for several nights after that, but they never saw it again.

She continued her letter, "Please find out where this animal came from and who it belongs to. It shouldn't be loose like this, someone will get hurt." She said she didn't want "any fuss or people with guns traipsing behind our house. We live near I-75 and I'm afraid this orangutan could cause a serious accident if someone hit it." She closed by saying, "Please look after this situation. I don't want my backyard to turn into someone else's circus. God bless. I prefer to remain anonymous."

The sheriff's office notified the Animal Control Division, which in turn contacted David Barkasy, the owner of the Silver City Serpentarium in Sarasota and a recognized animal welfare specialist. When shown the Myakka photos, as they came to be called, Barkasy was, of course, greatly interested. Aware that a professor in Maine, Loren Coleman, had written several books on cryptozoology and was considered a leading authority on the subject, Barkasy wasted no time in contacting Coleman. Through the chain of events that followed, serious studies of the smallest details of the photos led Coleman to issue a statement saying that they were perhaps "the first good non-hoaxed photographs of a so-called Florida Skunk Ape," but he added, "Further investigations must be ongoing."

Barkasy and Coleman made every effort to locate the woman who wrote the letter to the sheriff's office, but to no avail. They wanted to learn where the pictures were taken in order to do a thorough examination of that area, but unfortunately, the letter writer never came forward. She was apparently determined to maintain her privacy.

The Skunk Ape, Florida's version of Bigfoot, Sasquatch, the Loch Ness Monster, Yeti, or a host of other mysterious creatures reported to have been sighted in many parts of the world, is described as a humanlike, bipedal creature, seven to ten feet tall, covered with shaggy, dark hair, and having, some say, large, fiery-red eyes. The ape is said to have a prominent brow ridge and a low forehead. Invariably, a smell most foul, akin to rotten eggs, spoiled cheese, and animal excrement is described, supposedly caused by the creature living in air pockets of below-ground alligator burrows. Casts made of its footprints are sometimes as long as twenty-four inches and four inches wide, with anywhere from four to six toes. The Florida Skunk Ape's prints apparently do not show signs of knuckle walking as some other Bigfoot trails have demonstrated.

Early Native American tribes have versions of humanlike giants in their histories, particularly in the Pacific Northwest. In Florida, most but not all of the reports come from the Everglades region. Even before European explorers arrived, Florida's native Seminoles and Miccosukees talked of "Shaawanoki," meaning big hairy men. Creatures in other areas are occasionally described as emitting a foul odor, but with Florida's creature, the stench is a given, leading to the name Skunk Ape.

Scientists in general are not convinced that the Skunk Ape really exists, although some remain open-minded about the existence of a Bigfoot creature. One of the best known is British primatologist Jane Goodall, probably the world's leading chimpanzee expert, who has publicly declared her hope that the Skunk Ape does exist, while recognizing that there is no evidence at present to completely support such an idea.

The term *cryptozoology,* first coined in the 1950s, has come to be used in science to mean the study of animals not yet formally recognized by scientists but bolstered by evidence of some kind from human beings in the form of reports, anecdotes, and sightings. These elusive, unknown animals are called cryptids.

The International Society of Cryptozoology, which was formed in 1982 but forced to disband in 1998 due to financial difficulties, was a scholarly operation dedicated to the "investigation, analysis, publication, and discussion of all matters related to animals of unexpected form or size, or unexpected occurrence in time or space." Its aim was to evaluate evidence of animals whose existence is unproven and to create a forum where people could exchange information to be studied and evaluated. The society held its meetings at the Smithsonian Institution in Washington, D.C., with membership open to laymen and scientists.

The majority of the scientific community is generally skeptical of the Skunk Ape's existence, due to the lack of firm physical proof. They mainly credit sightings either to hoaxes or to misidentification of creatures already known. Volumes of evidence do indicate that multiple hoaxes have been fashioned over the years, but still, they do not provide indisputable proof that an undocumented animal does not dwell among us.

The most well known authority on Bigfoot, Loren Coleman, a professor at the University of Southern Maine, has followed various kinds of Bigfoot sightings for more than forty-five years. He estimates that 70 to 80 percent of sightings are hoaxes, but even so, he reminds us that new animals are being discovered every day. For example, as recently as 2010, a never-before-seen six-foot-long lizard was discovered in the Philippines, and in the last ten years, four hundred new creatures have been found—insects, birds, and mammals.

Of all the Bigfoot sightings, about one-third of them have been in the Pacific Northwest. There is even a charming tavern near Mount Rainier called The Bigfoot Tavern with a popular drink named the Red Eye and a resident band called The Howling Wood Knockers, in tribute to characteristics ascribed to the resident Bigfoot.

Some Floridians are convinced that the state's Bigfoot, the Skunk Ape, does exist because, for one thing, they question why any con artist would ramble through the steaming jungles of the Everglades or the Green Swamp, in Florida's heat and humidity, wearing a hot, furry gorilla suit, particularly during hunting season. Still, as we all know, people have been known to subject themselves to far worse when possible fame and fortune are involved.

Even so, it is probably best to consider the aim or motivation of those claiming to have seen a Skunk Ape. Are they trying to sell a book? Drum up publicity for a money-making scheme of some kind? Get personal pleasure out of putting something over on others?

Or, are they sincere people with no ax to grind? There have been countless accounts from reportedly honorable, forthright people who are totally convinced they encountered a Skunk Ape. Some may want to share their stories but fear being taken for a fool. People with flawless reputations, including professionals, officers of the law, and even scientists have described seeing the creatures while camping, hiking, or driving through some of the thousands of miles of Florida wild lands.

A group of upright, all-American Boy Scouts claim that a huge, hairy, apelike creature terrified them when they were camped in the Ocala National Forest in 1959. More than one long-distance truck driver has sworn to have experienced night-time encounters with large, smelly beasts when they pulled over to rest along I-75, Florida's western interstate. In 1971, a group of archaeologists saw a big, odoriferous ape in the Big Cypress Swamp. The creature left behind seventeen-and-a-half-inch tracks where it had walked.

The clearheaded and practical pastor of the Fort McCoy Baptist church in Charlotte County near the Lake Woodruff National Wildlife Refuge reported seeing a huge, hairy creature while he was driving on an unpaved road after cutting some firewood. In 1993, two different accounts of big, hairy creatures in the Titusville area were made public, one from a Lockheed Systems manager at the Kennedy Space Center and the other from a NASA engineer.

In 1997, two similar statements were taken from longtime residents with homes "grandfathered" within the Big Cypress National Preserve. The first report came from a well-known Everglades City real estate agent who had seen many bears near her home in the past and was certain what she saw that time was not a bear. She made her report reluctantly, knowing full well the sort of reactions it would generate.

The second sighting came from a one-time US Air Force intelligence officer, then chief of the Ochopee Fire Control District, whose home was near the home of the real estate agent. The fire chief, who was driving on the same road as the real estate agent's sighting, managed to get a photograph of the elusive ape-like creature, but the photo was not clear.

It is not always easy to screen out the hoaxes from the honest mistakes or misidentifications because, for one thing, the extent to which some folks will go to grab the limelight can be astonishing.

One recent Florida scam was a whopper in which a trio of Georgia hunters claimed to have in their possession the iced 230-pound body of Bigfoot. The three claimants were a police officer, a corrections officer, and a man with his own radio show, who openly touted himself as head of a firm devoted to solving the mystery of the creature, but whom some authorities described as nothing more than a con man. On television news networks, the men showed photos of their creature's frozen corpse and claimed to have DNA evidence to back up their statements.

However, eventual examination of the dead animal by a reputable biologist produced the DNA of a possum, apparently added to a dummy for odor effect. The Bigfoot corpse was a fake made with manufactured hair and rubber feet. Nevertheless, it seemed like a good way to sell Bigfoot T-shirts and caps; additionally, for just five hundred dollars, the men offered to lead adventurers on a Bigfoot expedition. The same radio host would later conduct an elaborate expedition into Florida's Thousand Island area in search of the Skunk Ape; he reported finding a huge "bedding area" and very large footprints, but alas, no Skunk Ape.

Regardless of the obvious hoaxes, the Myakka pictures were seriously studied, with videographers enlisted to analyze them. Biologists were consulted to consider whether the creature might be a feral orangutan. A PhD candidate in zoology measured and analyzed the size of the creature's pupil in the first and second photos. Others analyzed the animal's facial expression as it made the "whoomp" sound, according to the woman who sent in the picture.

While there was admittedly no assertion as to the validity of the photos, Coleman stated that he believed the photographs were neither of a person in a costume nor of a zoo animal that had escaped. He helped track the two photos to a specific photo lab. The FBI then consulted police, who had been dispatched when the anonymous letter was received. A Sarasota newspaper claimed that hairs found in bushes in the area did not match any known ape, but no follow-up was reported.

Ochopee, a small town on the Tamiami Trail surrounded by the Everglades, seems to be the area most preferred by the Skunk Ape. Given the human population of just 128 and bragging rights to the smallest post office in the United States, it is perhaps understandable that any shy, retiring animal might favor this area in Collier County. The locality also claims the only Skunk Ape Research Headquarters in the world.

The headquarters, run by brothers Dave and Jack Shealy, is also the front office for the Shealys' Trail Lakes Campground. The setup might remind visitors of some other small tourist

Skunk Ape Research Headquarters

attractions in the Sunshine State, complete with a petting zoo and the ubiquitous souvenir shop selling ice cream, T-shirts, alligator heads, Skunk Ape souvenirs, and other knickknacks.

As might be expected, the Skunk Ape Research Headquarters has attracted its usual share of skeptics, but Dave, the more outgoing brother, has been interviewed by the *Wall Street Journal,* the *Miami Herald,* and *Reader's Digest* and has appeared on the Discovery Channel, *Inside Edition,* and Comedy Central's *The Daily Show,* among other television programs.

Shealy claims that he has observed the Skunk Ape three times, the result of this determined man sitting in a tree for several hours every night for eight months, watching, waiting. To lure the Skunk Ape, he left mounds of what he says is the creature's favorite food, large half-dollar-size lima beans, which he soaks in water and scatters in piles about the area. (How he learned the creature preferred lima beans has not been explained.) When he finally glimpsed the creature one night, he sat back and watched, swearing he was never afraid. He was convinced that the animal, whatever it was, meant him no harm. The few photographs he took with his ever-present camera were not distinct enough to convince most observers of the creature's authenticity.

One favorite point that skeptics make is to ask what has become of the bones of dead Skunk Apes, if the creatures ever existed. Everything must die, so why have their skeletons never been found? It's not a hard question to answer, in Florida at least. In the Sunshine State's subtropical heat and humidity, even panther or bear skeletons are rarely found, either; in fact, rodents and other animals usually destroy the remains of other dead animals within twenty-four hours. Although the remains of the Skunk Ape would be much larger, there is no reason to believe its fate would be any different. In addition, Florida's subtropical climate would be a natural living environment for primates, as would the enormous wild areas in the state.

Another important explanation for Skunk Ape sightings that doubters offer is misidentification. The bear could easily be mistaken for the elusive animal, they believe. The bear stands upright, is hairy and dark, and inhabits areas where Bigfoot sightings have been reported. Their footprints are similar, and some humans who have been fairly close to bears say that most bears also emit a foul odor.

There are skeptics in the scientific community, but there are believers, too. Dr. Jeff Meldrum, professor of anatomy and anthropology at Idaho State University, has pronounced the search for Bigfoot to be a valid scientific one and is quoted as saying, "Given the scientific evidence that I have examined, I'm convinced there's a creature out there that's yet to be identified."

Jimmy Chilcutt, of the Conroe, Texas, Police Department, a prominent fingerprint expert, has studied the dermal ridges of men and apes and their distinct differences. After studying the casts that have been made of tracks thought to be from the Skunk Ape, Chilcutt put his reputation on the line by stating that the casts indicated the existence of an unknown primate.

According to Professor G. W. Gill, president of the American Board of Forensic Anthropology, professor emeritus at the University of Wyoming, and a widely recognized expert in skeletal biology, "Either the most complex and sophisticated hoax in the history of anthropology has continued for centuries without being exposed or the most manlike and largest nonhuman primate has managed to survive in parts of North America and remains undiscovered by modern science."

On the other hand, a Washington State zoologist, John Crane, has stated unequivocally, "There is no such thing as Bigfoot. No data other than material that's clearly been fabricated has ever been presented."

Nevertheless, every year scientists discover many new species. Some are small insects, but in 2010, they uncovered sizable animals like the aforementioned six-foot-long lizard and a red-bearded monkey that not only is the size of a cat, but also emits a kitten-like purr when snuggled. Loren Coleman reminds skeptics that it took almost seventy years for live specimens of the mountain gorilla and the giant panda to be found.

Interest in the Skunk Ape waxes and wanes. Sightings increase in frequency, then drop off but never completely disappear. Visitors continue to stop at the Skunk Ape Research Headquarters in Ochopee for Skunk Ape T-shirts and alligator teeth. The Bigfoot Field Researchers Organization, with its video cameras and microphones and other up-to-the-minute equipment, continues to offer expeditions to Skunk Ape fans—no guns allowed.

Currently, a film crew has begun work on a television documentary on the Florida Skunk Ape. It will be broadcast on the well-known Discovery Channel. Most folks in Ochopee are hoping the elusive star of the show will make an appearance.

CHAPTER 2

First American Civil Rights Martyr

Christmas Day was always special for Harriette and Harry T. Moore, but in 1951, there was an extra reason to celebrate. It was their twenty-fifth wedding anniversary, a milestone in their loving marriage.

Four miles west of Cape Canaveral, with a population of one thousand and not a single traffic light, the tiny town of Mims, Florida, glittered with Christmas lights on small, Cracker-style houses. Harry's mother, Rosa, had come from Jacksonville to join the family celebration, and the Moores' daughter Peaches was home from Ocala where she taught school. Her sister, Evangeline, would be home from her job at the US Department of Labor in Washington, D.C., on December 27. The family spent Christmas Day quietly, catching up on family news. They planned to open presents when Evangeline arrived.

Harriette, Rosa, and Peaches piled into Harry's car about four o'clock on Christmas afternoon for the drive through the orange groves to Harriette's mother's house. It was only about a half mile away, but the road was unpaved, which made walking difficult. Early in their marriage, Harriette's mother, Annie Simms, had given her daughter and new son-in-law an acre of land adjoining hers and her husband's, and there, the young couple built their home.

This day would be even more special because Harriette's brother, George, was home on leave from the army after an overseas tour of duty. Fifteen people, friends and family, planned to celebrate the day together.

There were three teachers in the family now that Peaches had followed in her parents' footsteps, but although Harry considered education important, especially in the black community, he was also active in organizing African Americans to register to vote. In 1934, he was instrumental in organizing the Brevard County chapter of the NAACP. Among the friends gathered together that Christmas Day was Elmer Silas, cofounder of the Brevard County NAACP, and he and Harry had much to talk about. One topic they discussed and felt strongly about was the discrepancy in salaries between black teachers and white teachers.

Briefly dismissing from their minds the spread of racial hatred and the incidents of violence in Florida, the group focused on the good feelings of comfort, contentment, and peace that filled the Simms house that day. The joyful celebration began to break up at 6:30 p.m., and at 7:30, Harry drove his family home.

Peaches retired to her old bedroom, and Harriette joined Harry in having a piece of fruitcake as a kind of celebration of their anniversary. They reminisced for a time, professing their everlasting love for each other before Harriette pleaded fatigue and retired.

Before she departed for the guest bedroom, Rosa took her son aside, pleading with him to stop his civil rights work. He was her only child, and she worried constantly about the dangers he faced every day. Even though he was forty-six years old, he hated to disregard his mother's wishes, but he remained convinced that it was something he had to do.

At 10 o'clock, Rosa turned in for the night in the guest bedroom at the rear of the house. Harry locked the doors, turned out the lights, and quietly joined Harriette in their bed.

At 10:20, the night—silent no longer—was convulsed by an explosion so powerful that it was heard all the way to Titusville, and so shattering that many immediately assumed something catastrophic had gone wrong with the missiles at Cape Canaveral.

Rosa barely escaped before the bedroom ceiling light came crashing down onto her bed. She had just started to breathe again when she heard the anguished cries of her granddaughter. Through the darkness, she ran to her and together they made their way to the master bedroom. Rosa nearly fell into the huge crater blown into the floor, where Harry and Harriette were half-buried under ripped floorboards and fractured furniture. Peaches frantically tried to dig her dazed, incoherent mother from under the rubble while Rosa clawed her way through the mess to find her son, who was barely breathing.

Peaches's involuntary screams pierced the night. Her uncles, Arnold and George Simms, lived fairly close by but slept through the explosion. Their frightened wives, who had been jolted from sleep by the blast, hustled their men to dress and hurry to the Moores' house—or, as it turned out, what was left of it.

Arnold and George were sickened to find one corner of the house blown off, windows shattered, shreds of wood and debris everywhere, and Peaches nearly hysterical.

The uncles worked hard to get Harriette and Harry out of the pit and into Arnold's car. The nearest hospital was thirty-five miles away in Sanford, but none of the family had telephones to call for an ambulance. Titusville was closer and had an ambulance, but it was for whites only. So, together with George, his brother who had served his country in Japan and Korea, Arnold barreled over the dark, foggy highways to Sanford with two barely alive relatives.

The Moore home in Mims, Florida, after the explosion

STATE ARCHIVES OF FLORIDA PRO1544

They made it to the hospital, but just as they arrived, Harry groaned loudly and blood gushed from his mouth.

When Harry, a native Floridian, had graduated from Florida Memorial College with a "normal degree," he accepted a job teaching fourth grade in Cocoa's black school. The job paid a small salary in the small town, but it was worth it, he always said, because there he met the love of his life, Harriette, another teacher. She added to her paltry salary by working as an agent for a life insurance company. Once they met, they wasted no time, marrying in 1926.

That fall, when Harry took over as principal of the Titusville Colored School and taught ninth grade, they moved to Mims, where Harriette's family lived.

Annie Rosalea, or "Peaches" as they called her, was born in 1928, and the young family built their home on the land given to them by Harriette's family. Harriette brought her sewing machine and her piano from her family home. Harry brought his books and planted a garden.

When Peaches was six months old, Harriette returned to teaching first grade at Mims Elementary, teaching until she stopped to give birth to Evangeline in 1930. Six months later, Harriette returned once more to teaching at the Mims school, feeling fortunate to be able to leave the girls in their grandmother's care.

Harry was a soft-spoken man whose mannerly demeanor coexisted with a strong determination to fight against racial injustice. Having started the Brevard County NAACP in 1934,

Harry was also active in the Florida State Teachers' Association (FSTA). He felt driven to solve the problem of the disparity between the salaries of black teachers and white teachers. Based on its own constitution, the NAACP was unable to be involved in politics, so Harry and others founded the Progressive Voters' League to handle those actions. Harry was a busy man.

He worked long hours, attended evening meetings, and traveled in his car around the state to encourage others and to advance black rights. One of the most important contributions he made was in getting blacks to register to vote. Eventually, the percentage of registered black voters in Florida was dramatically higher than in other Southern states, largely thanks to him.

It was not something most people wanted to hear, but during World War II, while blacks were dying in service to their country, they were discriminated against when they came home. As they began to demand their rights, a noticeable backlash took hold, including an upsurge in Ku Klux Klan activity. Lynchings occurred with greater frequency, and Florida took a shameful lead, surpassed only by Mississippi and Georgia.

In 1945, five short weeks after V-J Day, a black share-cropper in Madison, Florida, who threatened to expose a white landowner for overplanting his tobacco allotment, was shot and lynched. The press exploded in outraged protests, with Harry in the lead, demanding "vigorous action." He seconded a call to the governor for the suspension of the sheriff investigating the case because of the officer's ineptitude and the appearance of his possible collusion in the crime. To no one's surprise, the sheriff was cleared. The annoyed governor ignored Harry's persistent calls.

Then in 1949, a seventeen-year-old white farm wife, Norma Padgett, accused four young black men of raping her in Groveland, Lake County. An ugly white mob rampaged through Groveland's black neighborhood, recklessly shooting and setting fires, forcing the governor to call out the National Guard. Rampaging hordes of men from adjoining counties joined the locals, all armed. As a precaution, Groveland's 350 African American citizens were evacuated to Orlando. Sheriff Willis McCall quickly ordered a ban on the sale of guns, ammunition, and alcohol.

Five days later, a grand jury indicted the four young men who would become known as the Groveland Four, a sad tip of the hat to the Scottsboro Boys of Alabama.

Nevertheless, because of the reputation McCall had earned for his crass treatment of blacks, no one considered the sheriff a knight in shining armor. He was widely quoted as saying, "I don't think there is any question about it that the white race is a superior race to the black race. I believe that's a proven fact. In their native country, they're still eating each other. We don't do that."

As the situation calmed somewhat, Harry Moore sent a telegram to Governor Fuller Warren, urging prosecution of the leaders of the violence against black citizens, including the ones responsible for burning several homes. The head of the National Guard and others joined in, urging action on the part of Sheriff McCall, who (not unexpectedly) refused.

Three of the young suspects were captured and jailed in the local prison, but the fourth, Ernest Thomas, escaped. McCall led a posse into the woods, quickly cornered the young man, and killed him in a volley of gunfire. Investigations by authorities pronounced the Thomas death a "lawful homicide."

Back in Groveland, an all-white jury convicted the three remaining defendants, Walter Irvin, Sammy Shepherd, and Charles Greenlee, who all claimed they had been nowhere near Groveland when the crime took place; instead, they insisted they had been in an Orlando nightclub.

Irvin and Shepherd were sentenced to death. Due to his age, Greenlee, who was sixteen years old, was sentenced to life in prison. The three were transported from the local jail to Raiford State Prison.

Stepping up his labors, Harry Moore loudly demanded action and raised money for an appeal. Preparations were begun for another trial when the US Supreme Court overturned the convictions, ordered a retrial, and characterized Florida's conduct in the case as a best example of "one of the worst menaces to American justice."

Accordingly, on November 6, Sheriff McCall drove his unmarked black Oldsmobile to Raiford to pick up Irvin and Shepherd to return them to Lake County for their trial, which was to start the following day. By the time they started the 125-mile trip back, over the narrow, rural roads, the skies were dark.

Sheriff McCall stopped his car at a lonely spot on Highway 146. Without dawdling, he emptied his gun into his manacled prisoners, killing Shepherd and severely wounding Irvin.

McCall would claim the men, who were both handcuffed, had attacked him as they tried to escape. He shot them in self-defense, he insisted, adding that he hated to do it.

Two panels investigated. Both agreed that the sheriff had had no choice.

Sheriff McCall thought that would be the end of it, but he was badly mistaken. A widespread national protest erupted, one of the loudest voices belonging to Harry T. Moore. He deluged Governor Warren with telegrams calling for McCall's suspension and demanding that he be indicted for murder. Warren mostly ignored Harry, but others did not.

Harry's plate was full at the time. Not only was he spending a great deal of time on the McCall business, but he was also still putting in long hours for the NAACP, without getting paid for it. In addition, some higher-ups in the NAACP actively worked against him. A major bone of contention was a plan by the NAACP to raise dues for state members. Harry insisted that no one could afford to pay more and that members would leave the organization if the dues escalated.

The NAACP ignored him and, in the process, took away his position as state secretary. Harry had developed into an accomplished, respected organizer, which became obvious when it was quickly apparent that he was right about the dues increase.

Members who simply couldn't afford higher dues dropped out in large numbers.

It was a bad time in Harry's life, and it was about to get worse.

Even without his NAACP position, Harry kept on working for the good of his people. In a conversation with a friend who told him he needed to slow down because no one liked to be pushed. Harry said, "I'm going to keep doing it, even if it costs me my life. Jesus Christ lost his life doing what he thought was right, and I believe the Lord intended for me to do this work for the colored race. I may live to be a ripe old age or I may be killed tomorrow, or next month, or perhaps never, but I intend to do this until the day I die."

He was a quiet man, considered stern, but patient and always ready with a smile. Since he was not a good public speaker in the early days, he prevailed upon his daughter Evangeline to give his speeches for him. However, with the passing years, he overcame his nervousness. As he traveled around the state in his car to promote voter registration, Harry became fairly well known. He spoke to many groups, his face becoming familiar to many. Where he lived was not a secret, either.

So it was on Christmas Day in 1951 that, while a large group of Ku Klux Klansmen was enjoying a barbeque a few miles away, the Moores made preparations to join their extended family and friends for a quiet celebration.

While people may have known where Harry lived, it was surprising that someone would know which was his bedroom. Someone knew that he would not be home for the afternoon and early evening when the fog moved in. Someone knew exactly where to plant a bomb that would blow Harry through the ceiling and nearly bury Harriette under the pile of rubble that used to be their home.

Arnold Simms, with his loaded makeshift ambulance, barreled through the fog and the blackness to the emergency room at the hospital. They made it, but by midnight, Harry was dead. Harriette, incoherent and only half conscious, was unaware that the love of her life was gone.

Evangeline's sad homecoming on December 27 did at least give her sister, Peaches, some family to cling to. Rosa, as she had feared for a long time, attended her son's funeral. Harriette, badly injured, saw she had no reason to live and lasted just nine more days.

News of the Moores' deaths caused another explosion. This time it was a nationwide eruption of protests, meetings, and memorial services. Governor Warren was inundated with protests, as was US President Harry Truman.

The anger and outrage focused on Florida was underscored when eleven other race-related bombings that had taken place in the state that year came to light. FBI agents flew in from Washington, D.C., to investigate the Moore murders.

The clamor sounded all the way to the United Nations where Eleanor Roosevelt was forced to defend her country in the U.N. General Assembly. Many vacationers who formerly traveled to Florida decided to travel elsewhere.

The NAACP, without mentioning that it had recently fired Harry, organized an enormous memorial rally in New York City, where the famous poet Langston Hughes read a poem he composed to honor Harry.

In February, Walter Irvin was tried a second time. It took less than two hours for another all-white jury to find him guilty and again sentence him to death, provoking more angry protests. Even so, Sheriff McCall won reelection to a third term in a landslide victory. The combination of these events left many people shaking their heads and certainly caused the flood of bad publicity to continue.

An extremely thorough FBI investigation involved wiretaps, interviews, and even a mock-up of the bombing of a replica of the Moores' house. A grand jury subpoenaed Ku Klux Klansmen from surrounding counties to testify. In the process, it came to light that the Klan was responsible for a whole host of unspeakable crimes, many centered in and around Orlando.

After legal maneuvering, appeals, and delays, the Florida Department of Law Enforcement finally closed the investigation in April 1992, and the Moore case fizzled and died. There were no formal announcements; it simply no longer occupied center stage. The case has never officially been solved, although there are suspicions and unproven conclusions, mostly Klan-related.

Joseph N. Cox, a Klansman, committed suicide after being interviewed by the FBI, and he had apparently given no previous indication that he had considered taking his life. When he was dying of cancer, Edward L. Spivey, another Klansman, implicated Cox. Klansman Earl J. Brooklyn, who was recognized as being especially prone to violence, had floor plans of the Moore home in his possession when he was investigated. Tillman H. Belvin, also known as a particularly violent Klansman, was a buddy of Brooklyn's and hung out with him. Although the FBI was suspicious of all of them, none were ever arrested and all are now dead.

In 1955, Governor Leroy Collins, citing the many faults and errors in the Groveland case, commuted Walter Irvin's death sentence to life imprisonment. Irvin was paroled in 1969 and moved to the Miami area, but on a one-day approved visit to his family the following year, he dropped dead of an apparent heart attack. There were suspicions of foul play in some quarters, but it was never pursued. It was never proven that Norma Padgett lied about being raped, but she had submitted no evidence or witnesses to support her charges.

On the strength of his handling of the Groveland case, Willis McCall became a hero to segregationists and seemed to enjoy spending most of the rest of his life in one altercation after another. He was investigated forty-nine times in his career, was reelected seven times, and lost on his eighth try because, at the time, he was being tried on murder charges for kicking a black prisoner to death. He was acquitted and died at home in 1994 of a heart attack.

Peaches passed on in 1972, leaving Evangeline the only surviving member of the Moore family. She moved to be near her son in Washington, D.C., feeling depressed and somewhat bitter that her father, whom she adored, and her loving mother did not receive the recognition she believed they deserved. For after the first huge outcry, Harry and Harriette seemed to have been forgotten.

Harry T. Moore worked without pay and put his life in danger nearly every night for seventeen years for the good of his race. Yet, until recently, hardly anyone knew who he was. He did his work before the nation woke up, before the words of Martin Luther King Jr. were heard across the nation, before anyone had heard about Rosa Parks refusing to move to the back of the bus. Before the four little girls were murdered in the Birmingham church. Before Thurgood Marshall donned the robes of a US Supreme Court justice. Before the Florida Department of Law Enforcement held another investigation of the Moore case in 1991. No conclusions were reached, but the reopening of the case stirred interest in Harry Moore.

His hometown, Mims, named a street for him. The new Brevard County courthouse was named the Harry T. and Harriette V. Moore Justice Center. In 1998, Governor Lawton Chiles approved a grant to build a memorial park and museum, and it now stands on the site of Moore's exploded home.

In one of his last speeches, Harry said:

Freedom is not free. If we want our complete emancipation, we must be willing to pay the price.

Harry T. Moore, a man Florida can be proud of, paid the ultimate price willingly.

CHAPTER 3

St. Petersburg's Cinder Lady

Mary Hardy Reeser enjoyed her life in Columbia, Pennsylvania, population 12,000. As the wife of one of the town's prominent physicians, she loved playing the part of hostess in her large, nicely furnished home, decorated with antiques and her own meticulously crafted needlepoint. She filled her days with bridge and entertaining and providing home-cooked delicacies to her guests. She took pride in her only child, Richard Jr., who followed in his father's footsteps, graduated from Cornell Medical School, served in the military in World War II, and then settled with his family in St. Petersburg, Florida.

Mary stayed on alone in the family home for three years after her husband died, but in 1950, she decided to leave the town where she had been born and lived for most of her life. She wanted to be closer to her son and his family in Florida, where she found what looked to be the perfect studio apartment. It was in the Allamanda Apartments at 1200 Cherry Street, in northeast St. Petersburg. Mary quickly made friends with her other neighbors and with her landlady, Mrs. Pansy M. Carpenter, who lived in an adjoining unit. The neighbors all looked in on each other from time to time, complained to each other when it was called for, and helped one another when they were needed, just as her former neighbors in Pennsylvania had.

Although Mary loved being near her family, it soon became apparent that the move had been a mistake. Aside from missing her old life, community standing, and friends, the Florida heat in the summer months was so oppressive to her that she kept two fans blowing on her most of the time when she was in her apartment. The solution, she decided, would be to spend the warm season in Pennsylvania and the rest of her time in Florida. Some of her old friends who still lived in Columbia promised to scout around for a summer rental for her, and she was delighted with the plan. She couldn't wait to get back to Pennsylvania.

Her elation, however, was short-lived. As a result of a mild upswing in Columbia's economy, rentals had become scarce. After weeks of searching, Mary's two friends were unable to find anything suitable.

Mary's mental outlook plunged. She was sixty-seven years old, and she did not want to spend her golden years this way.

On July 2, 1951, hoping to lift her spirits for a while, she joined her son and his family for a midday Sunday dinner at their home. She enjoyed the afternoon babysitting her youngest granddaughter while Richard and his wife, Ernestine, spent time at the beach with their other two children.

It turned out to be a good family day, but Mary returned to her apartment early, quite obviously sad again. Because her depression had been so noticeable to her son and his wife, they each made a point to visit her at separate times for a few moments later that evening.

Her son was the last to stop by around 9:00 p.m. He later said that the last time he saw his mother, she was wearing her rayon acetate nightgown and robe, with the black satin slippers she customarily wore around the house. Mary was sitting in an easy chair with her usual two fans blowing on her and smoking a cigarette. She hadn't eaten any dinner, as she had no appetite for food, she said. She told him she had taken two Seconals and just might take two more later, to be sure of getting a good night's sleep.

Dr. Reeser kissed his mother goodnight, never dreaming that it would be the last time he would see her alive.

The smell of smoke awakened Pansy Carpenter at 5:00 a.m. Thinking it was probably coming from a defective water heater that had been acting up lately, she got up, went to the garage, turned off the pump, and returned to her bed. When she arose to start her day at 6:00 a.m., she set the coffee on to perk, opened the door to pick up her newspaper, and noticed the smoky smell was gone.

At 8:00 a.m. Pansy answered her doorbell to be greeted by a Western Union boy who said he had a telegram for Mrs. Mary Reeser, but Mrs. Reeser did not answer her door. Immediately concerned for her neighbor, Pansy took the telegram to deliver, but when she touched Mary's doorknob, strangely, it was hot, much too hot to touch.

She was not concerned anymore—she was frightened, frightened and terribly worried.

Not knowing what else to do, she ran outside and noticed some painters working on a building across the street. She called out to them, begging for help.

The two men hurried over at once, forced the door open, and walked into blistering heat, this even though the windows were open. One look at the blackened remains was all the painters needed. They closed the door and rushed Pansy to her unit to call the fire department and Dr. Reeser.

The firemen who arrived at the scene at first thought that no one had been inside the apartment until they saw a foot sticking out of the ashes. It was a horrifying sight even to men who were

Reeser Morgue photo

COURTESY OF LARRY E. ARNOLD; *ABLAZE! THE MYSTERIOUS FIRES OF SPONTANEOUS HUMAN COMBUSTION*

familiar with tragedy. Gritting their jaws, they forced themselves to get on with their job. With a small hand pump, the firemen smothered the few remaining cinders and a small flame that was burning on a wooden beam between the living room and the kitchen.

It was the beginning of the "Cinder Woman Mystery," which in some people's eyes has never been solved. An intense investigation involving fire officials, the St. Petersburg police, arson experts, and pathologists got under way without delay.

The grim scene that the painters had discovered was both horrifying and puzzling to everyone who studied it.

An area near the front window in one corner of the room, measuring about four feet by five feet, was incinerated, the carpet melted down to the cement floor. Centered in that area were the remains of Mary's large cushioned chair, burned down to the springs, and, beneath that was a blackened mass that was unrecognizable at first, then shocking and spine-chilling. There was a small mound of seared debris, mostly indistinguishable except for Mary's left foot at the end of it, the black slipper nearby. Closer examination revealed some of her vertebrae with burned liver attached to them and a rounded mass the size of a baseball that was assumed to be her shrunken skull.

The investigators were astounded. How did a 175-pound woman come to be reduced to less than ten pounds overnight inside her own mostly undamaged apartment?

Only the upper part of the walls of the room showed a line of smoke and oily soot and the upper portions of the drapes were thick with soot. Electrical wall outlets and plugs above a four-foot level had melted, which had caused a fuse to blow and, in turn, caused an electric clock to stop at 4:20. But closer to the floor on those same walls, similar electric materials were intact. Extreme heat had cracked a mirror ten feet from the burnt chair and melted two pink candles about twelve feet from it. Part of a cigarette lighter was pulled from the rubble. Only two legs of an end table next to the chair remained, and the lamp that had been on top of it was badly damaged. Certainly, the fact that the walls and the floor of the apartment building were concrete would have had much to do with the fire not spreading.

Much of the remainder of the apartment looked undisturbed. The sheets on a sofa bed were turned down neatly, as if ready for someone to retire. The clock still worked when it was plugged into another outlet. A stack of newspapers near the damaged area showed no signs of being scorched. Perhaps strangest of all was that intact left foot, burned off to about four inches above the ankle, the black satin slipper next to it.

When the coroner, Edward T. Silk, looked over the remains and scrutinized the apartment, he felt the death was accidental and ordered the charred fragments, ashes, and severed foot be taken by ambulance to the hospital.

St. Petersburg Police Chief J. R. Reichert, who had witnessed many fires, flatly stated: "This is the most unusual case I've seen during my almost twenty-five years of police work in the city of St. Petersburg."

Dr. Wilton M. Krogman, a professor of physical anthropology at the University of Pennsylvania's School of Medicine, who was visiting in Bradenton at the time and had previously investigated more than thirty fire deaths, was consulted. He said, "I cannot conceive of such complete cremation without more burning of the apartment." The world-renowned expert further stated, "I regard it as the most amazing thing I have ever seen. As I review it, the short hairs on my neck bristle with vague fear. Were I living in the Middle Ages, I'd mutter something about black magic."

Dr. Krogman went on to dispute the idea that the rounded mass some had identified as Mrs. Reeser's shrunken skull was actually her skull. "In fact," he said in describing other cases he had seen, "the opposite has been true. The skulls have exploded into hundreds of pieces or been abnormally swollen." He added, "The head is not left complete in ordinary burning cases. Certainly it does NOT shrivel or symmetrically reduce to a smaller size. In presence of heat sufficient to destroy soft tissues, the skull would literally explode in many pieces. I have never known any exception to this rule."

Because of the strangeness of the case, the FBI was called in to begin what would be a lengthy investigation by its agents and its laboratory, including painstaking analysis of bits of bones and other substances from the fire.

Inevitably, the story spread like the eye of a hurricane through the neighborhood and beyond, becoming ever more distorted as it did. The more melodramatic reports of the "shrunken human skull" fascinated the public, and people from all over wanted to join the hordes of reporters who descended on the scene.

Supermarket tabloids were beside themselves and undoubtedly helped to spread the crowd-pleasing explanation called Spontaneous Human Combustion (SHC), which is said to occur when a human being bursts into flames from a chemical reaction within it, without being ignited from an external source. Although some things such as a pile of oily rags or a pile of sawdust can spontaneously burst into flames, most members of the scientific community dispute the validity of SHC.

However, believers in SHC would point to the portion of the FBI report, which found "no signs of oxidizing chemicals, petroleum hydrocarbons, or other substances used to initiate or accelerate combustion." The account added that "common substances such as gasoline, alcohol, kerosene, or ether, would probably be burned up and leave no trace behind." It was also pointed out that some substances detected in the rug in the apartment were melted fatty tissue.

Since Florida is known as the Lightning Capital of the World, some thought the source of ignition might have been lightning. In fact, the police department did consider that possibility but concluded that "although there was a slight electrical disturbance on the particular night involved," there was "no indication in this case where lightning struck the building in order to kill the victim and set the body on fire. In most cases lightning leaves telltale evidence, either of entrance or exit."

Whatever the cause of SHC, hundreds of cases have been reported over the years, the first known one in 1663 in Paris. In the 1800s, Charles Dickens even used SHC to kill off a character in one of his novels, *Bleak House*. Subscribing to the accepted belief at that time that SHC was due to excessive alcohol in the body, Dickens made his character an alcoholic to make his demise more believable.

A more recent case that affirmed the theories of SHC supporters occurred in 1966 when the body of ninety-two-year-old Dr. J. Irving Bentley was found in his bathroom at home, incinerated to a pile of ashes but for his single unharmed leg and slippered foot. A hole in the bathroom floor where his body was found was the only part of his house that was not intact.

Most other accounts of SHC have been similarly described, and in nearly all of the cases, one or two extremities remained untouched by the fire. People who have studied this particular aspect of these cases often likened the extremities to logs, pointing out that any time logs are burned—in a fireplace or at a campfire, for example—the distal ends of the logs might still be there the next morning when the fire is out because fire does not burn well laterally. In Mary Reeser's case, she had suffered from a stiff leg and usually sat with it stretched out in front of her. Her foot was found burned off a bit above the ankle, much as a log would have burned. Also, it has been pointed out that very little fat is found in the lower extremities, particularly in the ankles and feet, so there is not much melted fat to fuel the fire.

The condition of the victims' remains in these cases is usually attributed to a phenomenon called the "candle effect" or "wick effect," referring to the "wick" being on the outside rather than on the inside, like a standard candle wick. With the wick effect, the victim's clothing burns quickly, igniting the body inside it. The burning body melts adipose tissue or body fat, which acts as a fuel and burns well since it is being absorbed into the chair or whatever the unfortunate person happens to be resting on. The chair burns and melts more fat and so on until the destruction of the body is complete. When there is no more fat to melt, the fire goes out.

The phenomenon was said to have been successfully demonstrated in a laboratory with a pig carcass, but the researcher has not been identified, possibly because of the potential for unpleasantness with animal rights groups.

Funeral directors and owners of crematoriums have differed somewhat in their estimates, but all offer that for a body to be burned as Mrs. Reeser's was, temperatures of 1,500 to 3,000 degrees Fahrenheit would be needed for two to three hours. Believers hold that SHC fires are small, do not spread, would never reach that intensity, and as such, are unnoticed and may go on for hours.

Most everyone agrees that human fat burns readily, and at five-foot-four and 175 pounds, Mary Reeser was plump. One highly respected authority, Dr. Lemoyne Snyder, medical-legal consultant to the Michigan State Police and a member of the American Medical Association and the American Bar Association, has stated that, contrary to popular belief, the human body is not resistant to fire. He has said, "Underneath the skin is a layer of fat which may be quite thick in heavy individuals. This burns readily and the destruction of tissue after a comparatively small fire may be great. . . . In many cases it seems the destruction of tissue by burning is out of all proportion to the intensity of fire which caused it."

In the case of Mary Reeser, it is not hard to see how the "Human Combustion" part of the equation could have occurred without the "Spontaneous" part. As her son, Dr. Reeser told investigators, his mother was wearing a rayon acetate gown and robe, which would be highly flammable if ignited. She had taken two sleeping pills on an empty stomach, and she mentioned that she might take more. Her depression had been interfering with her sleep, and she felt she needed the help of medicine. When Dr. Reeser last saw his mother, she was smoking a cigarette and sitting in a large cushioned chair (a perfect wick), with two running fans aimed directly at her.

When he arrived at his mother's apartment following her death, he was met by the fire chief, who happened to be a former patient of his. During their conversation, Dr. Reeser said he was convinced that because his mother had taken two Seconals, she must have fallen asleep while she held a lighted cigarette. The cigarette set the upholstery of the cushioned chair aflame. Since she was overweight, the flames fed on her considerable body fat. It was that simple. To him, there was no mystery. He left that to others.

The world still waits for proof of either the existence or nonexistence of Spontaneous Human Combustion, but some commonalities occur in many of the reported cases. More victims have been women, who have more body fat. Also, they frequently outlive men and thus live alone, so nobody is there to be alert to the situation. The episodes occur more at night and in winter when there might be more sources of flame. In many cases of SHC, alcohol and occasionally drugs have been consumed. A few victims were believed to have been physically impaired, making an escape from sudden flames impossible.

The mystery of Mary Reeser's death has been examined and debated on television programs and in books. Her ashes were examined and tested before being flown home to be buried in Chestnut Hill Cemetery in Mechanicsburg, Pennsylvania, next to the grave of her beloved husband.

Her son, Dr. Reeser, smiled when he claimed his mother's ghost remained behind in Florida with her surviving family. His family's guest room was furnished with items from Mrs. Reeser's Pennsylvania home, and he swore that he and his family occasionally smelled his mother's perfume, "L'heure Bleue," in the guest room. They claimed it was a nice, comforting feeling, not spooky at all. Even the children were comfortable with their Grandma's ghost.

The telegram the Western Union boy tried unsuccessfully to deliver on that fateful morning was from her two friends in Pennsylvania. They sent her the good news that they had found her a summer rental.

CHAPTER 4

The Trial of Ruby McCollum

I t was 1952. Ike Eisenhower and Adlai Stevenson were running against one another to become the next president of the United States. *I Love Lucy, Arthur Godfrey,* and *Dragnet* were among the top ten shows on television. A complete Chinese dinner at the House of Chan in New York City sold for $1.59. In the South, silence protected the widespread acceptance of the myth of white supremacy. In a small Southern farming town in north Florida, public and individual silence shrouded the shocking mystery of why a wealthy black woman shot and killed the town's highly esteemed white doctor and state senator-elect.

Live Oak, the Suwannee County seat, is a short distance north of Gainesville and about halfway between Tallahassee and Jacksonville. It is surrounded on three sides by the Suwannee River, the same river celebrated in song by Stephen Foster, even though he never ventured there.

On Sunday morning, August 3, 1952, while most Live Oak citizens were attending services at either the Baptist or Methodist church, the town's leading physician, Dr. C. Leroy Adams, was busy attending to patients in his segregated office not far from the Methodist church.

Meanwhile, Ruby, the wife of Sam McCollum, the wealthiest black man in the county, had secured her two youngest children in the backseat of her light blue Chrysler before driving from her home to the alley behind Dr. Adams's office where the entrance for black people led inside.

A young man waiting for his mother in a truck parked nearby saw Ruby walk to the office entrance several times, look inside, then return to her car, probably, he thought, to keep careful watch on her children. Finally, she stepped inside the door marked COLORED WAITING ROOM, walked past the few seated patients who were waiting to be seen, and confronted the doctor in an unoccupied treatment room.

The patients in the waiting room could not help but hear a terse, nasty exchange, including some mention of money, between the overweight, six-foot-two doctor and the petite, five-foot-three woman.

Suddenly, the Sunday morning calm was disrupted when three shots blasted through the quiet and the big man crashed facedown onto the floor, with a one-hundred-dollar bill clasped in one of his hands. The sound of another shot pierced the air, sending the screaming patients fleeing from the building.

Her mission complete, Ruby dropped the .32-caliber Smith & Wesson back into her purse, returned to her car, and drove home to feed her children. Calmly, she waited for the police, knowing they would arrive soon.

Police from all over Suwannee County immediately poured into the area around the McCollum home, and in less than an hour, Ruby was being ushered out through the gathering crowd.

Before many minutes had passed, the entire congregation of the Methodist church was aghast to hear the news announced from the altar that their well-known fellow member, Dr. C. Leroy Adams, had been murdered by a black woman.

Sam McCollum heard the shocking announcement at the Colored Baptist Church, where he and his eleven-year-old daughter were attending services. He stifled his horror, managed to hustle his child outside, and sped home before any members of the congregation could confront them. All the way home, he struggled to maintain his self-control for the good of the child. Soon enough, she would hear about the horrible scandal involving her mother.

Ruby McCollum was born and raised with six siblings in Zuber, Florida, an unincorporated speck on the map near Ocala. In 1929, she married Sam McCollum, and after living for a few years in New York and for a short time in Fort Myers, Florida, the young couple settled in Live Oak, where Sam joined his brother, Buck, in managing a lucrative bolita gambling ring. Bolita, a game imported from Cuba, consists of betting on small numbered balls and was popularized in Florida's Ybor City.

In Live Oak, the McCollums raised their family in one of the finest homes in Suwannee County. Ruby dressed fashionably in clothes from Jacksonville's best stores, furnished their home in the latest styles, and saw to it that their three daughters and son, Sam Jr., wanted for nothing. For those times, it was a remarkably good life for a Southern black family, although a precarious one in hidden ways.

Bolita was illegal in Florida, but it was well known that gambling was hugely popular in Suwannee County. Sam, who came to be called "Bolita Sam," was the boss of the operation in the area for fifteen years, overseeing the "writers" who worked the routes, taking bets, paying winnings, and keeping records. Some estimated the weekly bolita take to be in the thousands of dollars. Certainly, there was no way such a major business could survive in a place with such a small population without the covert approval of local law enforcement, but in Live Oak, that was not a problem.

Dr. C. Leroy Adams was from a formerly wealthy family in nearby Jasper, population less than two thousand. He married young and worked for the Works Progress Administration (WPA) before running unsuccessfully for Hamilton County sheriff. After obtaining a pharmacist's certificate in Florida, he opened a drug store that failed and then moved to Arkansas, where he worked in another drug store while he took two years of premed classes. He then attended the University of Arkansas Medical School, graduating last in his class.

With his wife, Florrie Lee, and their young son, the new doctor moved to Florida and set up his practice in Live Oak, determined to claim the area as his own. A man of great appetites, he made no secret of his extramarital dalliances, one of which involved Ruby McCollum. Even if he had wanted to hide, he most certainly could not have, what with the nearly three hundred pounds he packed on from endless overeating.

Adams made house calls all over the county at nearly any hour, refusing payment when he knew the patients were destitute. All he asked was that they have a chicken leg or two and some good, strong coffee ready for him when he finished caring for their family member. Word got around. The whole town talked about how he took care of everyone, made house calls at any hour, never made an issue of money—a truly noble man, everyone said.

His reputation grew to the point that by 1952, he gloried in being chosen the state senator-elect for three Florida counties: Suwannee, Hamilton, and Lafayette. At last, Dr. Adams seemed to be achieving the life he felt he deserved. He had a wife who was willing to put up with him for the sake of the good life he provided her. Their daughter, Laverne, was happily married to the head teller of Live Oak's local bank. And their son, Clifford Leroy Adams III, who had entered the military, was more than content with his choice.

In February 1952, the one dark shadow in the doctor's life occurred when his and Florrie's only son, on leave from the Air Force, was killed in an auto accident. To his patients, the doctor appeared devastated.

But by April, Dr. Adams was campaigning once more. His future looked bright, not only because Florida state senators were well paid, but also because the position was frequently a lead-in to the governorship.

What people didn't talk about was the hidden Live Oak and the doctor's dark side.

No one talked about the fact that Suwannee County was a safe haven for the Ku Klux Klan or that some local members of the Klan were looking forward to the prestigious jobs they rightfully expected when their comrade, the doctor, took office in the state legislature.

Swept under the table, too, was the time in 1949 when Dr. Adams was indicted for the phony bills he turned in to the Veterans Administration. He was found not guilty after he rounded up dozens of friends, including a former governor, and talked them into testifying as to his sterling character before the jury.

There were no public discussions either about how, when Blue Cross and Blue Shield began operations at Suwannee County Hospital, where Dr. Adams was essentially in charge, unnecessary surgeries were common, extraordinary amounts of supplies were being billed for, and patients were kept in the hospital longer than in other hospitals. Many of Dr. Adams's same adoring patients would tell anyone who listened that their doctor took such good care of them, often "for nothing," oblivious to the fact that he was collecting big fees from their insurers.

There was also the matter of Dr. Adams being in collusion with the local sheriff and most local law enforcement officials, who accepted generous payments for their silence and protection of the county bolita operations, Sam McCollum's lucrative setup. The only records showing how this high-stakes money changed hands (with none going to the Internal Revenue Service) were in the account books kept by Ruby McCollum. That the woman who owned those records was now in their hands, and only she knew where her account book was, must have caused considerable uneasiness among the authorities.

There was also the matter of the six-year relationship between the doctor and Ruby. It began when Dr. Adams took care of Ruby after a single episode in which Sam had struck his wife, resulting in some nasty bruises and abdominal pain that required X-rays. That was when Ruby first joined the doctor in illicit rendezvous and became the frequent recipient of the shots Dr. Adams was known for dispensing in Live Oak.

In the beginning, armed with the knowledge that Sam had had a few dalliances, Ruby had to feel some satisfaction at being chosen by Live Oak's leading citizen, but with her, it didn't stop there. Adams, who came to be known as the "shot doctor," so freely gave injections to Ruby, that she eventually reached the point of a true addiction.

Their relationship, which resulted in the birth of a fair-skinned baby girl named Loretta, was based on the Southern common-law view of "paramour rights." It is an unwritten law, protected by both black and white silence, dating from pre–Civil War days and lasting long afterward, that allowed white men to take black women as secondary wives and force them to bear children. At the time of the doctor's murder, Ruby was pregnant with his second child.

When she begged Adams for an abortion, he threatened to shoot her if she dared to kill his child. His children would live, he said, no matter what their color. Sam, her husband, had already told her that if she ever had another light-skinned baby, he would shoot her. The richest black woman in Suwannee County faced a frightening dilemma.

Live Oak was a small town, but it teemed with no end of secrets.

For the safety of their prisoner, the arresting officers wasted no time. They drove Ruby more than fifty miles from Live Oak, all the way to the Raiford State Prison, rather than incarcerate her in the local jail. She would remain at Raiford until early September before being returned to the Suwannee County Jail, where reports that she had a spontaneous abortion spread swiftly. One of her lawyers, however, was convinced that unknown people had given her drugs to induce a miscarriage. The esteemed white doctor's name must not be sullied.

Sam, meanwhile, was frantic, seeing no way out of the impending disaster. He hurriedly bundled up his three daughters, filled suitcases with their clothes and the thousands of dollars he had hidden in the house, drove to Zuber, where Ruby's mother lived, and collapsed on a bed in her home. Sam Jr. was safely away at college—one less worry—but Sam's heart, which had previously given him problems, gave out under the added stress. He died in his mother-in-law's home the day after he arrived.

As expected, news of the Adams murder had quickly spread around the town. Most blacks stayed off the streets and out of sight, some resentful that one of their own was the cause of this trouble. Horrified white people crowded the streets, trying to understand, asking each other why. That was the mystery. Everyone knew who committed the crime, but no one could understand why.

They didn't know that, a few days before the killing, Ruby had been in the treatment room at Dr. Adams's office, pleading for an abortion. They didn't know that in a fit of anger, the doctor had refused, knocking the mother of his child to the ground. No one knew that the mysterious one-hundred-dollar bill still in the doctor's hand when his body was found was Ruby's. No one was aware that on Friday of that same week, Ruby had opened an envelope addressed to her husband to find a message with a bill for $117 from Dr. Adams's office. Only Ruby and Sam were present when she confronted her husband with her suspicions that the bill was almost certainly for an abortion for one of the women he had on the side.

The bits of conversation overheard by patients in the waiting room and the money clutched in Dr. Adams's hand added to the mystery. The doctor had never been one to hassle anyone over money. Moreover, the McCollums were known as people who always paid their bills on time or even early. Every piece of evidence only served to make the puzzle more difficult to solve.

In the meantime, the sheriff, himself a Klan member, pressed some of his furious fellow Klansmen into keeping peace on Live Oak's streets, where serious talk of lynching the accused killer of the esteemed Dr. Adams was being discussed. To a Klan member, a black woman murdering a white man—any white man, much less a leading citizen like Dr. Adams—was unacceptable, to say the least.

The doctor's funeral drew crowds from all over the county. Among the pallbearers were Klansmen, highway patrolmen, and the judge who would officiate at Ruby's trial. The local newspaper, the *Suwannee Democrat,* was reverential in its writings about Dr. Adams, stating that his "medical practice was the largest in the county, and it included the rich and the poor, the white and the colored. He was truly everybody's friend."

In December 1952, Ruby went on trial in the court of Judge Hal Adams (no relation to the doctor but rumored to be a Klan member). The judge made clear from the start that the press would not be permitted to have access to the accused, to avoid any hint of sensationalism or of having the trial conducted in the newspapers. Freedom of speech and freedom of the press were not mentioned.

Zora Neale Hurston, the black Florida writer who would become famous after she died, was assigned to cover Ruby's trial for the *Pittsburgh Courier.* She was certain it would become known as the trial of the century, in that it would be the first tribunal in which a black woman would have the opportunity to defend herself against a white man who exploited her. Zora thought it should certainly mean the end of "paramour rights." Instead, she was witness to the community accepting that Adams, who never dunned for payments, was murdered for a small medical bill by a fiscally generous woman known to pay bills promptly. The real story was not allowed to be told.

Zora later was frustrated and appalled at "the smothering blanket of silence" that not only protected the Southern myth of white supremacy, but also protected Suwannee County from "what the outside world would say about the trial." Live Oak's citizens, white and black, closed ranks.

The trial proceeded routinely, even quietly, until Ruby began her testimony. Frank Cannon, her lawyer, began asking her questions that, when answered, would not excuse her behavior but would reveal her motive and perhaps provide some justification for it. Thirty-eight times in all, when Ruby attempted to answer the question put to her, the state instantly objected, thus preventing even the slightest inference that her action was, if not justified, at least understandable. Thirty-eight times, Judge Adams sustained the objections. Finally, Cannon recognized defeat with the plaintive words: "May God forgive you, Judge Adams, for robbing a human being of life in such a fashion. I would not want it on my conscience."

No one expected the case to be dismissed, only conducted fairly. When Thelma Curry, Dr. Adams's nurse, was on the stand

and was asked about office billing procedures, she began to relate some details concerning the quarrel between the doctor and Ruby, which she had overheard. The nurse was immediately silenced by the state's attorney and dismissed by Judge Adams, who admonished her: "Get down and go back where you came from!"

Ruby's lawyers even possessed a statement she had written to them from prison in which she said that she and Adams had "carried on for six years" and that she had always been afraid of him, because when she made him angry, he would often give her shots and other medicine that "almost killed" her. Still, the all-white, all-male jury convicted Ruby of first-degree murder and sentenced her to death.

Ruby was incarcerated in the Suwannee County Jail for two years in solitary confinement. Her failing mental health was as obvious to the few people permitted to have contact with her as her dramatic weight loss—from 145 to 87 pounds.

Then in July 1954, the Florida Supreme Court overturned the verdict on the grounds that Judge Adams had "failed to be present at the jury's inspection of the scene of the crime," an oversight that violated state law.

A large segment of Live Oak's population most likely heaved a sigh of relief when, at her new trial, Ruby was judged to be mentally incompetent. She was ordered to spend the next twenty years in the Florida State Mental Hospital at Chattahoochee, an institution noted for its frequent use of electroshock and insulin shock therapy and for heavily medicating many patients with Thorazine. Live Oak's secrets would be safe.

Ruby's mental state continued to deteriorate noticeably. Soon, the memory of much of her previous life no longer existed for her. In 1971, when Florida enacted the Baker Act, Cannon, who had represented her for very little money, worked to have her released and moved to the New Horizon Rehabilitation Center near Ocala, where she spent her remaining days.

Ruby died of a stroke in the early morning hours of May 23, 1992, at the age of eighty-two. She was buried next to her beloved brother in the New Hope Baptist Church Cemetery.

Her name was misspelled on her death certificate, but still, she has not been forgotten. The Springtree Studio has announced plans to begin filming *The Ruby McCollum Story* in the Gainesville area, directed by Bill Duke and featuring a cast that is expected to include Burt Reynolds and Matt Lanter. As of this printing, firm dates have not been released.

CHAPTER 5

A Tale of Two Judges

This is a mystery story about two Florida judges. One, Curtis Chillingworth, was a good judge; some even said he was a great one. In the summertime, he and his wife, Marjorie, lived in their beach house in Manalapan, a tiny exclusive community at the southern end of Palm Beach. It was an area known as the vacation home of the Kennedys, the Rockefellers, and the DuPonts, and later on, as a vacation place for Donald Trump, Jimmy Buffett, Rod Stewart, and other sports, entertainment, and political celebrities too numerous to mention.

Chillingworth was the fifty-eight-year-old wealthy son of one of Palm Beach's founding families. After he graduated from the University of Florida, he was admitted to the Florida bar, graduated from the naval base at Key West, then attended the US Naval Academy and was commissioned to serve on the USS *Minneapolis* during World War I. He returned to Palm Beach at the war's end to practice law with his father. He became a county judge at age twenty-four and shortly thereafter was elected to be circuit judge, a powerful position he held until his death. Judge Chillingworth developed a reputation for possessing a no-nonsense, fair judicial intellect.

Having remained in the Naval Reserves, he was called to active duty during World War II. His impressive wartime duties included devising the strategy for the occupation of Germany.

The second judge involved in this mystery was Judge Joseph A. Peel, thirty-one years old, dark-haired, good-looking, and partial to showy white linen suits. Palm Beach's only municipal judge, Peel at one time was chosen as the Junior Chamber of Commerce Man of the Year. He and his wife, Imogene, made their home in West Palm Beach, originally the community that Henry Flagler had established for the workers he brought into the state to build and care for the beachside mansions of wealthy Palm Beach residents.

Peel, a native of West Palm Beach, was the son of Buck Peel, a well-known and popular owner of a small, local hotel. The flamboyant son was given to photographing scantily clad women posed in front of his diploma on the wall in his office. He loved displaying his riches and his authority, and was not bashful about declaring that he would most likely be governor of Florida one day. He drove a Cadillac while his wife drove a Lincoln Continental, all of which was most interesting since his salary as a judge was only about three thousand dollars a year and his law practice was modest at best. How then did he afford his lavish lifestyle?

Through his private law practice, which he was permitted to maintain while he served as judge, Peel met and represented people like Floyd "Lucky" Holzapfel, a West Palm Beach mechanic by day, a known criminal after dark. Peel learned that Holzapfel had begun his shady life as a teenager in California and had already been involved in two armed robberies, while Lucky was impressed that the judge was interested enough to learn so much about him.

As for Peel, he could not resist bragging to his new acquaintance about how powerful he was and how he used that power for his own underhanded purposes. The purposes? Collecting protection money from local rackets operators was one. He found working both sides of the rules of society could be most lucrative.

The unlikely pair hit it off. They were soon joined by George David "Bobby" Lincoln, a black owner of two poolrooms and several taxicabs, who was a force among blacks in his neighborhood. Bobby could look mean enough to cause almost anyone to break out in a cold sweat, but at other times, slouched in the driver's seat of one of his antiquated, rickety trucks, he looked like any down-on-his-luck man, looking to make a few dollars to survive.

The three men formed an unusual partnership structured about West Palm Beach's three main rackets: bolita, Loteria Cuba, and 'shine.

Bolita, the numbers game imported from Cuba, was gaining in popularity, particularly among the poor in West Palm Beach. Loteria Cuba is a racket run in the States but based on a legitimate lottery in Havana. 'Shine is simply short for moonshine, the illegal sale of liquor distilled and sold in large quantities, tax-free in Florida.

Peel, in his capacity as municipal judge, could authorize police raids on bolita or 'shine saloons, then have his partners warn the suspects in advance, for a hefty fee, of course. Or he could provide warrants with slight defects, but sufficient enough to provide anyone who was convicted with grounds for an appeal and acquittal, also for a fee. Then, too, he was in a position to deduct payoffs from whatever fines were collected—and he did. Meanwhile, his two partners took care of the physical labors involved in the scheme. While it was a lucrative setup for all three men, it allowed Judge Peel to bask in contentment with his upscale life.

Among Judge Curtis Chillingworth's many admirable qualities was that he was always on time, never late in calling for order in his courtroom. On June 15, 1955, however, he was due to preside over a case at 10:00 a.m. and the usually punctual judge was nowhere to be seen. A call to his home went unanswered.

Meanwhile, two carpenters who had been hired by the judge to repair several window frames at his home arrived there that same morning to find the sprawling cottage overlooking the Atlantic deserted. Perplexed when they saw the judge's car in the garage, the men eventually phoned his office staff, who made more futile phone calls, then notified the authorities. In view of the judge's reputation for punctuality, the authorities decided to have the police investigate.

When the police arrived at the Chillingworth home, they received no response to their knocks. They discovered the house door was unlocked, but there was no sign of the judge or of his wife. An overhead porch light had been shattered, with shards of glass sprayed everywhere. Drops of dried blood spattered the steps leading down to the beach, where countless footprints in the sand seemed to lead to and from the ocean. The police found two used spools of adhesive tape, one in the sand and one in the living room. The judge's car was in the garage with the keys still in the ignition. It was cold, indicating it had not been driven recently.

The police consulted with the couple's three adult daughters, who knew only that the last anyone had seen their parents was when they left a dinner party at the home of James Owners Jr., the Palm Beach tax assessor, at 10:00 p.m. the night before.

The afternoon newspapers declared the couple missing.

That evening, laboratory tests confirmed that the blood on the steps was the same type as Mrs. Chillingworth's, but still, that proved nothing. There were no clues. There were no suspects. There were no bodies. Where were the Chillingworths? The disappearance of the prominent couple was a mystery.

Just two years earlier, Judge Joseph Peel's life had been progressing according to his plan. The partnership with his cohorts, Holzapfel and Lincoln, was proving to be a winning one, a financial bonanza for all three of them. Peel, however, made a careless mistake in his law practice by representing both sides in a divorce case, a practice considered unethical conduct by legal standards. He was charged, but the judge of the Florida Circuit Court referred his case to Judge Chillingworth.

Judge Chillingworth

Well aware of Chillingworth's strict ethical reputation, Peel was beside himself with worry. Ordinarily, he would have been correct to assume the worst, but luck was with him this time. Further enhancing his reputation as a fair judge, Chillingworth let Peel off with a reprimand, "because of his youth and inexperience of counsel." The younger judge breathed easier.

Unfortunately, Peel subsequently involved himself in several more minor episodes that Chillingworth considered judicial misconduct. Undeterred and emboldened with passing time, Peel ran for reelection in 1954. He was victorious, his aspirations escalating to where the title of governor and a move to Tallahassee didn't seem so farfetched.

Then in early 1955, Peel committed another error, a more serious one this time. He failed to file the correct divorce papers for a woman, who, thinking she was divorced, married again and filed papers to adopt a baby. When the adoption agency began its routine pre-adoption investigation, no record of her divorce was found to exist and, to her embarrassment and dismay, she was pronounced a bigamist—an unknowing bigamist, but a bigamist nevertheless.

The case went to court, eventually ending up in the hands of Judge Curtis Chillingworth. Chillingworth had let it be known in legal circles that Peel would never practice law in Florida again if the younger man ever came before him on another disciplinary charge. Peel was aware of Chillingworth's vow.

Wealth, power, prestige, the governor's mansion—all of it would be gone. Peel was thirty-one years old, and the life he dreamed of might be over. He would almost certainly be disbarred. It would be useless to plead his case, knowing the kind of man and judge Chillingworth was. The future couldn't have looked darker.

There was one way out. Judge Chillingworth had to die. In desperation, Peel called his dependable partners, his good old friends, Holzapfel and Lincoln.

Holzapfel was uneasy at first, but when Peel threatened to resurrect some old, unsettled criminal charges against him, he went along with the plan. Lincoln agreed to help for a cut of the ten thousand dollars Peel promised.

Any hesitation they might have felt subsided. The large sums of money they each routinely took home were courtesy of their buddy and accomplice, Judge Peel. It was a considerable bundle, and without him, that gravy train would run no more.

The trio decided on a simple plan. They agreed they would kidnap Chillingworth and use a small boat to take him out in the ocean, where they would dump him over the side. There would be no body to dispose of, no witnesses, and if they did it right, no case. Their partnership would go on, and the money would keep right on rolling in.

Peel did his part by driving his partners around Judge Chillingworth's neighborhood to familiarize them with the area. He pointed out the judge from a distance, to be certain they would recognize their prey. The plan was for Holzapfel to ring the doorbell of the Chillingworth home, and when the judge answered, say his yacht was sinking and ask to use the judge's phone to get help. Peel even suggested Holzapfel wear a yachting cap to make the story more convincing.

It was just after dark on the night of June 15 when Holzapfel and Lincoln began executing their uncomplicated plan. They drove to Riviera Beach, where they picked up a small boat at the dock and headed out to sea. It was a calm, starry night, with the lights of Palm Beach clearly visible to the men, but they took more than an hour to reach a point offshore from the judge's home. When they came to where the Chillingworth house was clearly visible in the moonlight, they were confidant that it was the right one. There was even a porch light left on, easily seen from the water.

They beached the boat, tossed an anchor over the stern, and jumped over the side into the shallow water. Pausing, they tugged the anchor line to be certain the boat was secure, walked over the sand, and climbed the wooden stairs that led up to the Chillingworth house. While Lincoln hid in the bushes, Holzapfel, with the captain's cap on his head and a gun tucked under his belt, knocked on the door. There was no answer. He knocked again. Inside, a light switched on and the judge appeared, in pajamas with his glasses on.

After verifying that he was the judge, Holzapfel described his invented problem, asking to use the phone to call the Coast Guard. When the judge understandably hesitated, Holzapfel pulled out his gun, announced it was a holdup, and demanded to know who else was in the home. Only his wife, Chillingworth said quietly. Holzapfel ordered him to call her while he summoned Lincoln with a whistle and told his buddy to knock out the porch light with the butt of his gun. Lincoln did, dodging the spray of splintered glass.

Marjorie Chillingworth was fastening the belt of the robe she had pulled on over her nightgown when she appeared, in answer to her husband's call. Wasting no time, the intruders grabbed her and quickly, roughly tied up the couple, with their hands behind their backs. They forced them out of the house and down the wooden stairs to the beach, repeatedly striking each of them.

The judge was not a big man, and with his hands tied behind his back, he could do little against two armed thugs.

Desperately, Marjorie once let out a piercing scream but was instantly silenced when Holzapfel smashed her skull with his gun. He picked her up off the sand when she fell and carried her to the boat while Lincoln forced her husband into it. They started the motor and headed out to sea.

When they were about two miles offshore, Holzapfel turned the engine off. He tied some weights he had stashed in the boat to the woman's waist and motioned for Lincoln to help roll her over the side. "Ladies first," he said.

There was no struggle from her as her husband called to her.

"Remember, I love you," he said.

Her last faint words were, "I love you, too."

Then, a splash. Nothing more.

The judge resisted as best he could while Holzapfel tied weights to his waist. Even though his hands were tied, Chillingworth twisted vigorously enough that he managed to toss himself over the gunwale, trying to swim away from the boat. A crack on his head with the butt of a gun slowed, but didn't stop him, forcing Holzapfel and Lincoln to grab him, tie weights to his middle, and then watch while the judge sank along with the guns that they tossed over the side after him.

They watched the water long enough to be certain their mission was complete before motoring back to the Riviera Beach docks. Holzapfel immediately telephoned Judge Peel to let him know in a prearranged coded message that the deed was done.

Peel joined them as planned but was dismayed and shaken to learn that Mrs. Chillingworth had been at home and endured the same fate as her husband. Understandably upset, Peel was forced to accept that there was nothing else his buddies could do.

A thorough investigation by the sheriff's office came up empty. There were no bodies. There were no witnesses. The few clues amounted to nothing. There was simply the fact that a prominent judge and his wife had disappeared and nobody knew where they were or what happened to them.

Judge Peel's life and career went on. He continued to practice law after he abandoned his judgeship, but without that special influence he had enjoyed for so long. Nevertheless, his desire for money and the good life continued.

About two years after the Chillingworths' disappearance, Peel took out a significant life insurance policy on Harold Gray, a young lawyer who worked in his office for a time. The sole beneficiary of the policy, which included a double indemnity clause in case of violent death, was none other than Joseph Peel, attorney at law. Peel managed to pull off this shady deal through James Yenzer, an insurance agent with a dubious reputation.

When the unsuspecting Gray accepted Peel's cordial invitation to join him for drinks at a club one night after work, a waiting Holzapfel ambushed the young lawyer in the dark. Although Gray was beaten until he was near death, amazingly, he survived. When the facts came out, the heretofore extremely lucky Floyd Holzapfel was arrested, as were Yenzer and Peel on lesser charges. Almost unbelievably, Holzapfel was acquitted and the charges against Peel and Yenzer were dropped, but Peel did agree to resign from the bar.

The astonishing turn of events didn't stop there. In 1958, Yenzer and Holzapfel were hired as house detectives at a plush Palm Beach hotel. While working there, Holzapfel and Lincoln maintained their association in the 'shine business, to supplement the less than satisfactory income they earned.

Following some raids on several local stills, the two buddies concluded that a certain acquaintance, a stool pigeon by the name of Lew Gene Harvey, was responsible for tipping off the police. They lured Harvey to a deserted spot in the woods, shot him, and dumped his body in a nearby creek, probably thinking they had once been so successful with a watery grave that it would work again. This time it didn't.

The body surfaced, was discovered, and the police investigated. Clues led to suspicions, and eventually detectives learned that Holzapfel had bragged about involvement in the Chilling-worth killings. The dead case began to show signs of life.

The police arranged a setup in a hotel room with Yenzer, whose conscience was bothering him and who wanted to make amends, and a very sharp undercover agent, said to resemble Lil'Abner, named Henry Lovern.

As the conversation proceeded, lubricated with generous amounts of spirits, Yenzer began to brag in detail, and in doing so, implicated Peel. What he didn't know was that the police were taping their conversation from the next room.

Holzapfel was arrested on October 1, 1960, pleaded guilty to both murders, and was sentenced to death row, where he slashed his wrists but survived. Even though his death sentence was com-muted, he suffered great remorse, at one time stating, "People like us ain't fit to live. We should be stamped out like cockroaches." He died in prison thirty years later, a model prisoner.

Peel, too, was arrested and in 1961 was found guilty of acces-sory to murder. He received two life sentences, was paroled in 1981, but was ill with cancer by that time. The former judge with a killer's heart lived just a few days after being released from prison.

Bobby Lincoln, who had been given immunity in the Chillingworth murders and in the Harvey murder for his testi-mony, was incarcerated for an unrelated crime in Michigan. He completed that sentence in 1962 and died in 2004. Like Holzap-fel, Lincoln, too, slashed his wrists while he was imprisoned, but it was his only attempted killing that ended in failure.

The bodies of Judge Chillingworth and his wife, Marjorie, have never been found. Likewise, the guns reputed to have been tossed into the ocean after them have never been found, despite a search of the area by divers.

In 2011, in what might be considered an affirmation of the old saw, "An apple never falls far from the tree," a respected Palm Beach attorney, Clark Cone, was sentenced to five years in prison for grand theft and scheming to defraud. Previously disbarred, Cone was convicted of bilking large sums of money awarded to his clients who had been harmed by medical errors or illegal corporate actions. What has this to do with the tale of two judges? Clark Cone is the biological son of Joseph Peel. When his mother divorced his jailed father, she married another judge, Al Cone, a highly regarded West Palm Beach judge who adopted her two children by Peel. Joseph Peel Jr. became Alexander Clark Cone, but unfortunately, did not follow in his adopted father's footsteps.

CHAPTER 6

Escape from a Sea Monster

The morning of March 24, 1962, dawned beautifully in Fort Walton Beach, Florida—warm, clear, and sunny, the kind of morning travel magazines like to brag about. It would be a perfect day for scuba diving, sixteen-year-old Edward Brian McCleary agreed with his friend, Eric Ruyle, when he phoned. Three other friends were going to join Edward and Eric for a whole day of diving around a sunken ship near Pensacola Bay, a venture Edward had been eager to tackle for some time.

A native of Brooklyn, New York, Edward and his family had moved to Fort Walton Beach in 1961, and one of the things he enjoyed most about his new Florida home was diving. The thought of diving on a submerged ship conjured images of swimming through the clear, greenish-blue Gulf of Mexico water, beneath the ship's decks, through mysterious, open passages teeming with exotic fish, undersea plant life, and coral.

The dive would be doubly exciting, because the boys would be diving on the legendary USS *Massachusetts,* the oldest existing

American battleship, all 350 feet of it having been commissioned in 1896. Edward, who had boned up on some of the ship's history, knew that it saw its first battle way back in the Spanish-American War. The USS *Massachusetts* was decommissioned in 1919 and towed to Pensacola in 1921, where it was scuttled just outside the bay entrance, originally intended to be used as a target for experimental artillery. In the 1950s, when several companies made known their intention of using the ship for salvage, the people of Pensacola vehemently objected, the state filed an injunction, and the case eventually went before the Supreme Court. Pensacola citizens were delighted to learn the Court subsequently awarded the USS *Massachusetts* to the state of Florida, and it has remained a magnet for scuba divers ever since. Edward and his friends couldn't help but be excited about checking out this ship.

Eric soon arrived at the McCleary home in his battered Ford, accompanied by friends Larry Bill, Brad Rice, and Warren Sullay, all in their teens. The boys had a seven-foot air force rescue raft tied to the roof of Eric's car. The raft was equipped with oars, an anchor, and pockets in its sides for provisions. They planned to use it to paddle back and forth to the ship, which was about two miles south of Pensacola Pass.

During the little more than a half hour it took to drive to Fort Pickens State Park, the boys told the Florida newcomer, Edward, some bare facts about Fort Pickens. He learned that it was one of the few Southern forts to remain in Union hands during the entire Civil War and that it was the largest of the forts built to secure Pensacola. It had remained under military control until 1947, when it became a state park.

When they arrived at the park, the boys climbed up to where a telescope had been installed at the top of the main section of the brick structure. Using the telescope, they could see part of the object of their trip—the two gun turrets of the USS *Massachusetts* protruding from the sea.

The youngsters changed clothes, loaded up the raft, and pushed off into the cold, clear water, taking turns with the oars. The boy from Brooklyn was fascinated as he looked down into the water, and he knew he would gladly put up with the cold to explore that mysterious world below.

The USS *Massachusetts* was only about two miles off the coast, but as they rowed toward it, the seas unexpectedly began to churn. Under a sky that had turned gray, small whitecaps washed over the low sides of the raft so that, as hard as the boys paddled, they could make little headway against the increasing strength of the waves. One thing they most certainly did not want was to be pushed out to the open water of the Gulf of Mexico.

They all agreed they should turn around and head back to shore. Larry and Brad worked the oars, while Edward, Eric, and Warren jumped into the icy water to kick and help to push the raft forward. It wasn't easy and they were making almost no progress with the fierce wind, the tide, and the waves all working against them. Not only that, but in what seemed to be seconds, the waves grew so strong and so high that the three boys in the water were forced to struggle back aboard the raft and had to cling to the sides to keep from being thrown into the water.

As the skies continued to darken, it was plain to see that the small boats in the vicinity were heading back to their ports. The boys frantically tried to attract the attention of someone— anyone—hoping for some help. No one seemed to notice them until an elderly woman in a small Chris-Craft that was about to enter port looked their way. The five boys stood and waved their arms, frantically yelling, "Mayday! Mayday!"

When the woman smiled and waved, they were relieved, thinking surely she would alert someone and they would be helped. But their hopes were dashed as they saw the Chris-Craft proceed on its way and the woman never looked back.

Desperate, Brad grabbed a shark gun he had stashed in the raft. He fired a shot with his red shirt tied to a line affixed to the spear and aimed it directly at the small boat. It landed close enough to the boat that they thought it must have been seen by someone, but there was no response. The boys' hopes sank.

But not for long. This time it was Edward who came up with an idea as his eyes lighted on the buoy that permanently marked the USS *Massachusetts* in the water. The red, lighted bell buoy was just about a mile away and easy to see from where they were. He suggested they tie up to it to keep from being washed away. The boys agreed, and despite the high waves that were beginning to swamp the small raft, they somehow managed to paddle to it.

Up close, however, the size of the buoy was frightening. It was steel and it towered at least twenty feet over the puny raft, causing the water beneath it first to suck in, then to surge out in the other direction when it rocked violently in the waves.

The boys were all terrified, certain they were about to drown. There seemed to be no way out—until Edward came up with a last, desperate idea. He shouted to them that he might be able to toss the anchor and lasso it onto the buoy so they could hang on and not be carried out to sea until the weather calmed down. The others, hardly daring to hope, still encouraged him to try, but just as he attempted the toss, an undertow dragged the raft down to the bottom of the buoy, threatening to batter them. The panicked boys plunged into the churning water, desperately trying to avoid being crushed as the buoy smashed into the raft, forcing it several feet beneath the water's surface.

They looked around, counted heads, and saw that they were all there and that the raft had made it, too, surfacing a short distance away. They all swam for it. Then, using their hands and feet, they climbed aboard with great difficulty and hung on for dear life in the darkness as the needlelike rain pelted their skin. Before very long, panic set in again when they realized that their raft was being washed past the USS *Massachusetts* and that there was nothing they could do but hang on and wait and pray. And wait and wait.

Then amazingly, after what seemed like hours, the angry sea did quiet down some, the waves started to flatten, and they watched fog move in. It became strangely and blessedly quiet.

The air even seemed warmer, but with the fog, they could see no more than a few feet away.

Then suddenly, in the almost creepy stillness, a strange noise pierced the air. It didn't sound like a boat, they thought, but what was it? Almost at the same time, a most unpleasant dead-fish odor overwhelmed them, followed by a huge splash that sounded not very far away. They froze, waiting for whatever was going to come next.

There was another splash, and then they saw what looked at first like a telephone pole sticking out of the water. It appeared to be about ten or twelve feet long, greenish-brown, and shiny, and they could make out a sort of bulb on the end of it, almost like a head. After a few moments, the thing started to move, bent over, and dove under the water, leaving behind the incredibly foul odor that caused the boys to feel nausea along with their terror. When it dove, they thought they saw something like a dorsal fin on whatever the strange creature was.

Frozen in fear, they watched until all at once, a shrill whine shattered the stillness and the five panic-stricken boys grabbed their fins, jammed them on, and jumped from the raft into the water, with Edward and Eric in the lead. They swam wildly, not really knowing what direction they were headed because of the fog. All they knew was that the terrifying splashing and hissing noise was following behind and that they feared for their lives and had to get out of there. With their crushing, never-ending physical effort, they were soon near exhaustion, but they forced themselves to keep swimming until a scream pierced the air and Warren shouted that he needed help because "it" had Brad. Then Warren's voice stopped.

Edward, Eric, and Larry screamed at each other, trying to stick together, sick with horror, devastated to realize that Brad and Warren were gone. The three continued thrashing through the water, not knowing where they were or where they were headed, but then the fickle weather changed again. The fog began to clear, the waves grew higher, a chilly rain started to pelt them once more, and along with it, lightning seared the heavens. They were tired and frightened and suddenly, to their horror, Eric and Edward realized that Larry was gone. They dove down, trying to find him, but finally knew it was hopeless. He was gone.

Within minutes, Eric gasped, flailed as he swam to Edward, grabbed onto his neck, and held on, moaning with terrible cramps. Both were exhausted but knew they had to keep going. Desperately, the two swam together in the darkness for what seemed to be hours, still unsure if they were headed in the right direction or out to sea, and with Eric getting heavier and heavier and Edward more and more tired.

Then, there was a brilliant flash of lightning, and Edward was able to make out the outline of the wreck of the USS *Massachusetts* not very far away. Elated, with Eric still hanging onto him, Edward swam harder, coaxing Eric to keep trying to help. But as they neared the ship, a big wave swamped them, tearing Eric from his grasp. But Eric was swimming, Edward saw,

momentarily encouraged, until suddenly the long-necked creature rose out of the water, opening its mouth as it hurtled itself
on top of Eric. In one horrible instant Eric was gone.

Edward was alone. Nearly paralyzed with terror and exhaustion, his later memory of what he did or what happened next
was foggy. He thought he swam—he must have. He thought he
died— did he, for a while? In time, he didn't know how long it
was, he felt sand under his body and tried to walk, but it was so
hard to walk when he could barely move. Still he struggled on, an
inch at a time until he came to some sort of a tower and somehow
managed to drag himself up a ways before he lost consciousness.

He was aware of nothing more until the morning sun
awakened him, but even then he could barely move his aching
body. When he tried to descend a ladder, he collapsed onto the
sand. He forced himself to try again, struggling to stand and
walk, collapsing once more. Then out of nowhere, a gang of
young boys appeared and came close, peering at him intently.

Could he be one of the divers lost yesterday, they wanted to
know. When he nodded, mumbling in the affirmative, they told
him that the Coast Guard had found the raft and that a search
was on for the other divers.

If there was any more conversation, Edward did not remember it when he awoke later in the Pensacola Naval Base Hospital.

Sometime afterward, during a visit from the director of
the Search and Rescue Unit from the Pensacola Naval Base,
E. E. McGovern, Edward told him everything he could recall,

including what he could remember about the "thing" that killed his buddies. He left nothing out, even though he suspected no one would believe him, but the kind director listened respectfully. He told Edward he believed his tale, and before he left, he confided to the boy that he believed the sea had many secrets.

The Coast Guard physicians at the hospital estimated that the exhausted survivor had been in the sea for more than twelve hours. Although it could not be determined exactly, some in the Search and Rescue Unit guessed that he had swum five miles during his ordeal.

Although none of the bodies except one were ever recovered, Edward believed the one decomposed body that washed ashore a week later was that of fourteen-year-old Brad Rice. The others, he was sure, had been eaten by the monster. The raft the boys used was recovered ten miles away.

Edward was treated for exposure and shock at the Naval Base Hospital before being released to his parents; then he had to

USS *Massachusetts* BB-2

COURTESY OF MICHAEL W. POCOCK

face reporters. He never changed his story, always insisting that a real sea monster was out there and that it had killed his friends.

The nightmarish adventure eventually led to him suffering a nervous breakdown, but with his youthful stamina, he apparently recovered from it in three months. After a time, he refused to discuss the episode any further, and unconfirmed reports circulated that he later became an addict and an alcoholic.

Of course, there were skeptics who did not believe in the existence of a sea monster. That was to be expected. But if the adventure was fabricated, what could have been the reason? Certainly, Edward could have offered a more believable tale—a shark attack, perhaps. Or, the raft might have overturned in rough seas. But he stuck to his story—at least he did until he stopped talking altogether.

Some asked: If the monster was so inclined to eat bodies, why did it not eat the one body that washed ashore? And if the night was so dark, how was Edward able to see the greenish-brown color of the long neck? And in this tremendous age of technology, how could such a huge creature elude detection? Unanswered questions, all of them. Edward could not answer them, but he knew what he saw.

Despite the bizarre nature of Edward's story, scientists estimate that 80 percent of all life on Earth lives beneath the oceans, an excellent place to avoid detection. In addition, nearly three-quarters of our planet is ocean. Some experts have even calculated that, if Mount Everest were moved to one of the valleys in the Pacific Ocean, there would still be more than a mile of water over its tallest peak.

Since mankind actually knows more about the moon's surface than we know about the world's oceans, is it really so surprising that we may not know many of the sea creatures that exist? New ones are being discovered with surprising frequency. Until November 1976, no one was aware of the existence of the megamouth shark, a repulsive-looking twenty-foot-long creature with a huge mouth and more than one hundred rows of teeth. In the thirty-plus years since then, just fifty more of these creatures have been sighted or caught.

Scattered sightings of the giant squid were reported over many years, but in 1978, one was stranded, enabling scientists to study it. The largest one ever measured, its body was twenty feet long and it had thirty-five-foot-long tentacles, making for an impressive fifty-five-foot-long creature. The giant squid lives mainly in the deep sea and hardly ever emerges at the surface. Only carcasses have been studied, but the creature has been authenticated with the name *Architeuthis clarkei* in scientific literature.

Undersea robots have produced films of bizarre creatures in recent decades. Now, new ventures financed by some deep-pocketed adventurers, including James Cameron, director of *Titanic, Avatar,* and *The Abyss,* are planning dives in newly crafted submersibles, built in Florida, to the deepest parts of the Pacific Ocean—about seven miles down.

With much of the planet beneath the oceans unexplored, who knows what sort of creatures will be discovered? The cause of the deaths of those four boys may never be known; but then again, perhaps it will.

CHAPTER 7

Dead Zone on Interstate 4

The accident seemed to be an omen on that first day, when Florida's Interstate 4 was opened to traffic. It was definitely unfortunate for the driver who lost control of the tractor-trailer he was driving, causing it to jackknife on the length of highway that in time would become known as the I-4 Dead Zone. Whether or not one believes in omens, the high number of traffic accidents and fatalities dating back to the 1960s on this most heavily traveled section of I-4 is sobering to contemplate.

Interstate 4 is central Florida's only east-west interstate highway, although as it connects Daytona Beach in the east to Tampa in the west, it runs northeast-southwest much of the way. Originally, the main part of Florida that I-4 ran through was unsettled country. Walt Disney put an end to that when Disney World opened in 1971, but as early as the 1880s, another man exerted his powerful influence on the same area. His name was Henry S. Sanford, and in the years following the Civil War, when he was minister to Belgium, he invested in plantations in

South Carolina and Louisiana, and in twenty-three thousand acres of undeveloped land in Florida that bordered Lake Monroe. It was Sanford's hope to turn much of his Florida acreage into orange groves profitable enough that he might interest others to buy parcels of his remaining land and follow his lead.

To entice people to come to Florida, he founded a town he immodestly named Sanford and then set about constructing streets, a general store, a telegraph center, a hotel, and other necessary facilities. He oversaw the development of his namesake town while continuing to run his own plantation. Although he was a wealthy man, he badly overextended himself financially to the point that he needed to have his real estate pay higher dividends. With that in mind, in 1880, he joined with some other British and European capitalists to form the Florida Land and Colonization Company Limited. Sanford was named president and chairman of the company's board of directors, but the other board members and the main offices were in London, England. Sanford, who became known among many of his Florida associates as being ill-tempered and unmannerly, apparently didn't get along any better with his English board, according to rumors at the time.

Nevertheless, the town of Sanford continued to grow with thriving businesses, an increased population, three newspapers, and an opera house. By the time the population surged to 2,250 in 1886, the Baptist, Episcopal, Methodist, and Presbyterian churches were all established. The Florida Land and Colonization Company decided it was a good time to offer a desirable plot of land to the

Roman Catholic Church in hopes that it might break ground on a colony, which would be called St. Joseph's Colony. Henry Sanford wanted to attract as many German Catholic immigrants as he could to the colony, where he would sell them real estate.

Orlando's first resident priest, Father Felix Prosper Swembergh, was named to oversee the new colony. Shortly after he began his duties at St. Joseph's, however, he was needed in Tampa to minister to sufferers of a yellow fever outbreak. Unfortunately, Father Swembergh fell victim to the same disease and died while he was there.

Clearly, with only eight families having put down roots, St. Joseph's Catholic Colony was not attracting settlers as had been hoped. The disappointment mounted when an outbreak of yellow fever in the colony took one family, both parents and two children. The names of the families who had been in the colony were listed as Bauer, Forwald, Geiseker, Kreuppel, Kulsch, Ochbosch, Yueger, and Schlosser, but it was not recorded which family had fallen victim to the fever.

Hoping to stop further spread of the disease, the entire family was hastily buried in the woods. With Father Swembergh gone, there could be no last rites and no religious or memorial ceremony of any kind held. Furthermore, it was the end of the colony, the remainder of the settlers having hastily moved away, in hopes of escaping the dreaded yellow fever.

The one unfortunate family remained, buried in individual graves on colony land that, as time passed, would evolve into the town of Lake Monroe, named for the nearby lake.

Sign on Interstate 4

In 1905, a farmer, Albert Hawkins, purchased a large parcel of the land that had been part of the colony. When he cleared the area for planting, he came upon the four graves, identified with wooden markers that were weathered so badly that the names were illegible. Hawkins respectfully left the markers in place, farmed around the graves, and continued to honor them in this way for years.

Among themselves, the people of Lake Monroe referred to the tiny cemetery as the Field of the Dead.

Hawkins occasionally leased out sections of his lands to other farmers, always reminding them not to disturb the graves. It was rumored that one farmer chose to ignore the caution; on the very day he began removing the rusted and battered wire enclosure around the graves, his house burned down.

After Farmer Hawkins died in 1939, his widow held onto the property until 1960, when the government made known its desire to buy the land to build Interstate 4. By then, the elderly Mrs. Hawkins was ready to move closer to her grown children. Additionally, she was informed that the interstate highway would be important to the state of Florida, as it would be a big factor in enabling people to reach the attractions that were going to be built by Walt Disney. That she would be contributing to the growth of the state was a good feeling for an aging lady. To her, it seemed to be a win-win situation.

State surveyors were made aware of the four graves on the property, but since they were so old and there were apparently no descendents that anyone knew of, someone in authority decided that it would be simpler to build the new highway over the graves rather than move the remains away. The state not only refused to move the graves, but it also declined to place markers of any kind, declaring that the graves "are not historically significant." The cost of moving the graves, officials claimed, was a factor, when no relatives would assist financially. Accordingly, in September 1960, the first fill dirt was dumped over the graves to elevate the land for the new interstate.

September is the height of Florida's hurricane season, and in 1960, one of the all-time great hurricanes, Hurricane Donna—the only one on record that produced hurricane-force winds in Florida, the mid-Atlantic states, and New England—made her appearance, taking many lives and causing billions of dollars in damage.

Donna took an unusual path through the center of the state, nearly following the planned route of the new interstate. The storm crossed the state diagonally from the west coast of the peninsula, headed for the east coast, and on the way, it passed directly over the tiny cemetery outside Sanford at midnight on September 10. Although the widespread wreckage and flooding Hurricane Donna caused in Florida did not stop the construction of Interstate 4, it was responsible for a delay of several months. Was it another omen?

The legend of the I-4 Dead Zone, though, seems to have been cemented in Florida lore on that initial day of the highway's operation, when for unknown reasons, the driver of the tractor-trailer lost control of his vehicle and jackknifed it directly over the site of the graves. Whatever its cause and whenever it began, the eerie spirit of the Dead Zone continues to this day.

In a list of the most dangerous highways in the United States, Florida can claim two of the top three. The 382-mile stretch of Interstate 95 along the east coast of Florida takes the prize as the most dangerous road in the entire United States, with the most fatal accidents. New Jersey's Interstate 76 is the nation's second deadliest, but it takes just 132 miles of Florida's I-4 to capture the third spot, while the short stretch of I-4 in central Florida between Orlando and Daytona Beach is its most deadly. Some wonder, could those graves that were covered over have anything to do with it?

Over the years, many strange occurrences have been reported in the area that measures only a quarter of a mile or so. From ethereal beings hitchhiking at the side of the road to ghostly trucks and orbs making their way across the interstate—all have been reported, often by people not generally given to belief in the occult. Truckers, making delivery runs through the area, have frequently reported seeing one or more persons walking along the highway and then disappearing.

Disruptions in radios, cell phones, and even tape and CD players are common, with noisy crackling sounds interrupted by voices. Some truckers have reported hearing male voices demanding, "Who's there?" and sometimes childish female voices giggling. No one ever responded when the truckers tried to communicate with the voices. Two power plants not far from the I-4 Dead Zone could account for some of the disruptions, but could they explain the mysterious voices? Would power plants cause voices to ask, "Why? . . . Why?" or, "Who's there?" over the static?

One Florida trucker, who regularly hauls produce through the area, has experienced enough strange episodes that he admits he routinely locks his doors before he enters the I-4 Dead Zone. Another driver claimed that the only car accident he ever had occurred when his steering wheel locked, for reasons no one could ever determine, and he crashed into a guardrail, causing a great deal of damage to his car. The man admitted the incident made him a firm believer in the Dead Zone myth.

One woman swears she has been involved in just three traffic accidents in her entire life, and all three took place at the notorious spot on I-4. Another woman, who moved to Florida recently and admits to being "sensitive," claims that her discomfort was so acute when she traveled over the Dead Zone that she now avoids it, even though the detour adds considerably to her mileage.

People were understandably intrigued when a photo made its way over the Internet that showed a ghostly figure standing in front of a smashed vehicle on the same stretch of highway and there seemed to be no rational explanation for it.

With so much publicity given to the unearthly specters in the area, psychics and mediums have visited on occasion, some claiming to feel a coldness and a deep melancholy emanating from the ground where the family of four was buried so long ago. A few seers say they have heard voices arising from the surrounding undergrowth and from the nearby river. Some have even left floral wreaths near the spot where the graves were supposed to have been buried. Even so, the state of Florida shows no interest in marking the gravesite.

As the rate of accidents continues to soar, one Florida Highway Patrolman thinks the answer is plain and simple. Accidents are mostly caused by drivers who are distracted, and sources of driver distraction are on the increase with cell phones, navigation systems, video players, and all the other new gadgets so many drivers seem to think they cannot do without when they travel. Certainly, dense smoke from brush fires contributes to poor visibility during Florida's dry season, when hundreds of charred acres may be short distances from the highway. Driver vision is further reduced by heavy rains during the thunderstorm season in the Lightning Capital of the World.

Another distraction, one that is probably especially true for visitors and cannot be removed, is the sight of nearby Lake Monroe, a beautiful spectacle that acts as a magnet to anyone's eyes. Additionally, extremely short on- and off-ramps are also considered hazardous.

Even the economic recession can play a part in high traffic accident rates. There is a shortage of funds to repair broken pavement, inadequate signage, improperly working lighting devices, missing guardrails, and other worn-out or destroyed structures or equipment. In some cases, additional lanes might be useful when traffic increases by leaps and bounds, as it has in central Florida, particularly in the Dead Zone, but any dip in government finances makes all but the most imperative road work out of the question for the time being.

One individual who travels the Dead Zone frequently felt so strongly about the potential hazards of this particular stretch of road that he wrote a letter to the *Orlando Sentinel* that likely sums up the sentiments of many local residents:

I have just completed another commute on Interstate 4, and I believe it is my duty to report that the I-4 corridor is one or two months away from eternal and total failure.

If you think you must use I-4, be advised to carry adequate food and water to last until a rescue party can save you. Women with an unborn child, particularly if they are in their last two months of pregnancy, should avoid I-4 at all costs unless accompanied by a certified midwife or Lamaze partner.

Wearing a bulletproof vest and installing high impact glass in your car may not be a bad idea either.

—Fred Milch

Hopes were raised in some circles in 2010 when the Obama administration marked $2.4 billion as a federal fiscal stimulus to the state of Florida for an Orlando-to-Tampa high-speed train, which would have undoubtedly lightened the load on the interstate highways. Most experts thought that the rising costs of fuel alone would have persuaded people to ride the train rather than drive, and some were convinced that a high-speed train would have made badly needed money for the state from the first day of its operation.

However, due to many factors, including the current uncertain financial climate, the rail line has not become a reality. Traffic will continue unabated on I-4, at least until the nation's financial picture improves, or a future governor stands behind a high-speed rail line.

The fact remains that more traffic accidents occur on that particular quarter-mile stretch of highway than on all the rest of I-4 between Daytona on the east coast and Tampa on the west coast. It might be a coincidence. Or could it have something to do with the graves buried beneath it?

CHAPTER 8

One Small Step—or One Giant Hoax?

In 1969, three astronauts, all experienced test pilots, pre-pared for a journey never before undertaken by anyone in the history of the human race. The trio consisted of cool, calm Commander Neil Armstrong, thirty-eight, a Korean War jet pilot credited with previously saving the Gemini 8 space capsule from disaster; Buzz Aldrin, thirty-nine, a decorated Korean War fighter pilot with a doctorate from the Massachusetts Institute of Technology, who solved the spacewalking difficulties of the Gemini flights; and Michael Collins, thirty-nine, a lighthearted veteran of a Gemini 10 space walk and designated pilot of the command module during Armstrong and Aldrin's proposed moon walk.

After training eighteen grueling hours a day, spending the final month away from their families, and being isolated in quarters with three windowless bedrooms, these three American men and three thousand tons of Saturn rocket finally lifted off from the launch tower at Cape Canaveral. As they rose to the heavens atop a column of fire, they were supported by some four hundred thousand people, scattered across the nation, who were involved in the flight.

Millions more watched from around the globe, as much as one-seventh of the world's population. Nearly a million people poured into Florida, jamming the beaches as near to Kennedy Space Center as they could get, many having camped all night along US 1 with coolers, bug spray, blankets, and binoculars. Six thousand special guests of NASA crowded onto the Cape, along with eighteen thousand journalists from all over the world. Among NASA's invited guests were former president Lyndon Johnson and his wife, Lady Bird; Walter Cronkite; Charles Lindbergh; Jack Benny; Johnny Carson; 30 senators; 205 congressmen; and 19 governors. An estimated three thousand boats of all types anchored in the Banana and Indian Rivers near the Cape.

On July 16, 1969, the earth shook and the sand four miles away vibrated as all eyes fixed on the sky to watch the perfect Apollo 11 launch. *Columbia,* the command module, carrying *Eagle,* the lunar module, and three explorers were on their way.

On July 20, Michael Collins detached the *Eagle* from the *Columbia,* radioed, "See you later," and continued on alone around the moon, leaving his two colleagues, with Armstrong at *Eagle's* controls, to lower themselves onto the moon's surface. Upon discovering that the terrain at the planned landing point was covered with huge boulders, making landing impossible, the unflappable Armstrong quickly located another spot to safely lower the lunar module onto the moon's surface—with twenty seconds of fuel left in the tank.

Nearly the whole world watched the two men perform tasks that had been specified back on Earth—taking photos, collecting soil samples, fastening mirrors and other components to the moon soil for future experiments to be carried out from Earth, and seeing as much as they could in the precious two hours and twenty-one minutes they had scheduled for their stopover.

They departed reluctantly, leaving behind a plaque inscribed, "Here men from the planet Earth first set foot on the Moon, July 1969 A.D. We came in peace for all mankind."

The mission was a glorious success. Even the Soviets rejoiced, as did much of the rest of the world. Armstrong, Aldrin, and Collins came back to Earth to a heroes' reception.

With no time to waste, Apollo 12 shot off from the Cape a few months later and repeated the successful US moon landing. Apollo 13 circled the moon without landing because of an exploding oxygen tank but returned to Earth safely. Missions 14, 15, and 16 completed their moon landings triumphantly, and in December 1972, Apollo 17 accomplished extensive studies of the moon, all of which led proud Americans to use the phrase, "If we can put a man on the moon, why can't we . . ." time after time when problems seemed insurmountable.

However, no sooner had Neil Armstrong set his big, bulky boot on lunar soil than the skeptics were off and running, insisting that his footprint was made on the set of a soundstage or in a hanger on a secret military base. The whole event, some said, had been orchestrated by President "Tricky Dick" Nixon, who was known to have been involved in secret tapes and cover-ups and who knew what else. Since the United States needed to show the world that the Soviets couldn't beat us in space, the doubters asked, what would be better than claiming we landed men on the moon?

Apollo 11 crew (Armstrong, Collins, and Aldrin) conducts checks in the Command Module (69-H-957)

To most Americans who were alive in the 1960s, watching the moon landings on television was breathtaking. It was a never-to-be-forgotten experience, to be among the six hundred million other people around the world whose eyes were glued to television pictures beamed straight from the moon, watching human beings take the first steps on another body in the solar system.

Any time in history would have been a good one to participate in the wonder, the euphoria, the jubilation of actually seeing a man walk on the moon, but in 1969, after more than a decade of unrest and bad news, people all over the world, and especially in the United States, felt an uncommon sense of exhilaration and pride.

Back in 1957, when the Soviet-launched Sputnik had begun sending its signals back to Earth, the Space Race became part of the Cold War. The United States hastily launched a satellite program to gather valuable information while tensions increased. President Eisenhower, facing mounting political pressure, established the National Aeronautics and Space Administration (NASA) with the aim of fostering more discoveries.

However, soon after much of the nation took satisfaction in electing the young John Kennedy to be their president, the Soviets scored again, sending the first man into space.

NASA determinedly and somewhat hastily outlined a blueprint for its overall mission: Project Mercury would send an astronaut into space, Project Gemini would develop crew procedures and docking maneuvers, and Project Apollo would land a man on the moon and bring him back again.

NASA proceeded toward its goals with a crash program even while other disturbing events were going on all over the globe.

Our nation, still discomfited from the fiasco of the Bay of Pigs invasion, held its breath and prayed the world would not come to an end while JFK and Soviet Premier Nikita Khrushchev negotiated their way out of the Cuban Missile Crisis.

Then, without warning, the young president was dead, leaving behind these words, "I believe this nation should commit itself to achieving the goal before this decade is out, of landing a man on the moon and returning him safely to earth."

Accordingly, NASA continued to forge ahead with its plans, while the racial situation in the country grew more tense. Martin Luther King Jr. energized blacks and sympathetic whites to stand strong in the face of intense hatred and the murder of four little girls in a Sunday school bombing.

A climbing casualty list in Vietnam fed the swelling antiwar faction and sporadic riots. Drug use was on the rise, women demanded an end to sex discrimination. Assassins gunned down Martin Luther King Jr., Medgar Evers, and Robert Kennedy. President Johnson, bruised and wearied by the war and the riots, decided not to seek reelection. The United States' influence around the world sank. Despondent Americans wondered, "What next?"

In the meantime, conscious of the deadline explicit in JFK's memorable words and still smarting from the Soviets' long line of "firsts" following Sputnik—first man in space, first woman in space, first satellite circling the moon, first space walk—NASA went ahead full speed. The decade was more than half gone when the astronauts Gus Grissom, Ed White, and Roger Chaffee locked themselves into the Apollo 1, just as they would for a real launch, but on the ground for a demonstration test. A stray spark ignited in the capsule, completely filled with oxygen, ending the lives of three brave men and plunging all of NASA into its darkest hour. The entire nation mourned.

Morale was so low following this tragedy that the program could have ended there, at least for the time being. But JFK's words were not forgotten, nor were the prescient words of Gus Grissom, spoken a week before the tragedy. He said, "If we die, we want people to accept it. We are in a risky business, and we hope that if anything happens to us, it will not delay the program. The conquest of space is worth the risk of life."

Americans heard, and across the country, workers in the Space Race straightened their spines and buckled down, more intent than ever. They identified the disastrous problems by working on modules that had been intended for Apollo 2 and 3. They solved the problems and made some 1,300 changes before launching the three unmanned Apollos 4, 5, and 6.

In October 1968, just fifteen months before the target date of putting a man on the moon, astronauts Wally Schirra, Walter Cunningham, and Donn Eisele successfully orbited the Earth in the newly redesigned Apollo 7.

In December 1968, Frank Borman, Jim Lovell, and Bill Anders orbited the moon in Apollo 8, followed by Apollo 9 with the first manned test of the lunar module in 1969. Apollo 10, an important practice exercise of a lunar landing in May 1969, preceded the mission the nation eagerly awaited: Apollo 11.

Despite the successes, the hoax rumors started not long after the July 16, 1969, liftoff of Apollo 11. They multiplied dramatically in 1976 when a book, *We Never Went to the Moon,* hit the bookstores. Distrust of the government and belief that NASA still lagged in technology were so pervasive that the book was well received by skeptics.

Then in 1978, a sci-fi movie thriller, *Capricorn One,* further fed the anti-NASA sentiment with its unfavorable depiction of the agency and its portrayal of a faked Mars landing patterned after the real moon landing. The film was otherwise notable for starring two husbands (one current and one ex) of Barbra Streisand and presenting O. J. Simpson in a minor role.

Despite much evidence to the contrary, a list of theories to support the idea that NASA's moon landing was a hoax spread. Some of the explanations people believed then and now are that: (1) the moon landings were faked with the help of Walt Disney on a soundstage near Las Vegas, where NASA was in cahoots with the Mafia; (2) while Apollo 11 was lifting off, it was empty of astronauts, who were partying at the time in Las Vegas; (3) the Saturn rocket was dispatched by remote control into the ocean as soon as it was out of range of telescopes; (4) the astronauts were flown to the Hawaiian islands when they were due to return to Earth, put in a fake capsule, and lowered into the ocean from a military plane; (5) the photos the astronauts took with fake moon rocks were done with the assistance of Walter Cronkite; (6) director Stanley Kubrick aided in producing the special effects photos similar to those he created in the film *2001: A Space Odyssey;* and (7) moon rocks seen in photographs were molded in a kiln for NASA.

Those theories were only the beginning. Over and over, conspiracy theorists pointed out that in the photos, the American flag the men planted on the moon appears to be flapping in a breeze, but there is no air on the moon. Explanation: The flag appeared to move because it had just been fixed into the ground and inertia kept it moving as the picture was snapped.

"There are no stars in the photos!" The conspiracy theorists suggested the soundstage had a black background and someone forgot to paint in some stars. Explanation: The moon reflects sunlight, creating a glare that would have made stars invisible when the photos were taken.

Some of the photos Armstrong and Aldrin were supposed to have taken of each other had to be taken by someone else because neither man is holding a camera and supposedly just two of them were on the moon. Explanation: The astronauts had hard-to-detect cameras along with other paraphernalia attached to the chests of their space suits and simply pressed a certain spot on their suits for a snapshot—no aiming, no focusing necessary.

Various shadows come from different directions in some photos, so the light sources had to have come from various studio lights. Explanation: Light sources were reflected from the sun, the Earth, the lunar module, and the moon itself.

When Armstrong and Aldrin left the moon, they left behind the lunar module, the flag, several instruments to be used in further studies from Earth, and some mementos, including the aforementioned plaque. Doubters say that if this were true, instruments such as the Hubble Space Telescope should be able to see these objects; but they are not visible from any source. Explanation: At this time, there is no telescope powerful enough to reach the vast distance necessary to view anything smaller than a very large building.

There is a region above Earth known as the Van Allen belts and skeptics believe that astronauts passing through them would be quickly killed by radiation. According to NASA, our spaceships pass through the belts at tremendous speeds, and their tests demonstrate that the metal hull of the spaceships blocks all but very small amounts of the radiation.

Conspiracy theorists continue to come out of the woodwork, with some more successful at reaching a widespread audience than others. In 2001, Fox TV produced a one-hour program entitled *Conspiracy Theory: Did We Land on the Moon?* Besides presenting the hoax theories that had been circulating for twenty-plus years, the program convinced some skeptics that the United States planned to use this giant hoax to force the Soviets to finance their own lunar program, which would eventually cause their economy to collapse, along with their government.

Although NASA ordinarily ignores the skeptics, this time it issued a statement expressing its disappointment that some people continue to "ignore basic science principles to diminish arguably the greatest feat in the history of human exploration."

The astronauts who participated in the Mercury, Gemini, and Apollo programs have usually tried to avoid one-on-one interviews with known conspiracy theorists, but occasionally it has been unavoidable. In 2002, seventy-two-year-old Buzz Aldrin was lured to a hotel, supposedly to interview for a Japanese children's show. However, once there, he was accosted by a thirty-five-year-old, six-foot-two, 250-pound part-time film-maker who thrust a Bible in Aldrin's face, demanding that he swear he really landed on the moon. The 160-pound astronaut decked the man with one punch to the jaw and left. The police refused to pursue the matter. After all, they said, it *was* Buzz Aldrin.

Still, conspiracy theorists continue to assert various versions of their opinions, some implying a government connection to the Freemasons, some to the Nazis, some to aliens. Philip Plait, who has a PhD in astronomy, has debunked the hoax theories, saying the enormity of such a forty-year conspiracy just isn't believable. "You're talking about NASA keeping the most massive secret of all time." Indeed, it is hard to imagine how the greatest government ruse in history could go on for more than four decades and involve thousands of people with none ever divulging the secret.

It must be kept in mind, too, that nine of the twelve astronauts who walked on the moon from 1969 to 1972 are still alive, and all will swear to their adventures.

Then, too, those same twelve astronauts brought pieces of the moon back with them—841 pounds of rock in all. Scientists who have examined the specimens claim they are totally unique, differing from Earth specimens in countless ways.

Dr. Marc Norman, a lunar geologist, says that "lunar samples have almost no water trapped in their crystal structure, and common substances such as clay minerals that are ubiquitous on Earth are totally absent in moon rocks." Even nonscientists attest that there is something very unusual about moon rocks when they are held in the hand. Samples of the moon rocks have been shared with scientists all over the world, including some foreign scientists who would not especially want to go along with any US hoax, and none have ever disputed their source. Additionally, some scientists insist that the moon rocks are more than two hundred thousand years older than the oldest Earth rocks.

Besides bringing rocks back from the moon, the United States and other nations have, as of this date, left more than three hundred thousand pounds of equipment of one kind or another there. When lunar spacecraft launch and leave the moon, portions of them, which are empty of fuel, separate and fall. Pieces of scientific equipment, such as the mirrored reflectors left behind by Armstrong and Aldrin, are there, as are a few golf balls Alan Shepard let fly during Apollo 14. The men of Apollo 15 left behind a statue known as the *Fallen Astronaut* as a tribute to all those who gave their lives in the "great leap for mankind." Sooner or later, scientists will surely be able to photograph it all.

Landing a man on the moon cannot be separated from the entire space program, nor can the multitude of innovations we now enjoy because of our exploration of the heavens, including our visits to the moon.

Probably nothing has had a more widespread impact on our lives than computer technology. Of necessity, computers had to be reduced from the size of a three-car garage to a size that would fit in a space capsule, so that today we use tiny computer chips in everything from airplanes to cars, toasters, alarm clocks, cell phones, and toys. Smoke detectors, Dustbusters, and super-efficient foam insulation used in mattresses and football helmets were all first developed for astronauts. The Global Positioning System (GPS) helps pilots in the air, sailors out at sea, and drivers on the nation's highways know where they are to within ten feet. Highly flame-resistant fabric, a more efficient carbon dioxide detector, heat-resistant paint, an unsinkable life raft used in rough sea rescues, fireproofing material, concentrated baby foods, freeze-dried mixes, fabrics that protect from UV rays, ingestible toothpaste, and biofeedback techniques were all first developed for space exploration. Medicine has NASA to thank for much pioneering in space technology, including portable X-ray machines, programmable pacemakers, MRIs, devices to test and treat balance disorders, bioreactors that assist in stem cell therapy, and antigravity treadmills.

With the exception of one more journey, the Apollo mission was at an end, and an extraordinary end it was. In 1975, when the final Apollo command module docked in peace with its Soviet counterpart, a Soyuz spacecraft, the two crews met in the small connecting passageway. Mercury astronaut Deke Slayton warmly shook the hand of the Soviet commander, Alexei Leonov, high above Planet Earth. From that moment on, the space rivals would cooperate, even build and work together on space stations. The political race was over.

What did not end were the same lamentations of a vocal minority who continue, more than forty years later, to insist that the moon landing was all smoke and mirrors. Referring to them, Neil Armstrong has said, "One, people love conspiracy theories. They are very attracted to them. As I recall, after Franklin D. Roosevelt died, there were people saying that he was still alive someplace. And, of course, 'Elvis lives!' There is always going to be that fringe element on every subject, and I put this in that category. It doesn't bother me. It will pass in time."

CHAPTER 9

D. B. Cooper's Florida Widow?

In March 1995, Duane Weber, a Florida antiques dealer, was dying of polycystic kidney disease in a Pensacola hospital. Weak and no longer able to take nourishment, he motioned to Jo, his wife of seventeen years, to come closer. His voice was so faint she could barely hear him as she leaned over his hospital bed.

"I have something to tell you," he whispered. "I'm Dan Cooper."

The name meant nothing to her, as it would have meant nothing to most people at the time. She wondered, was he delirious? She knew he had spent time in prison under another name at least once, but the details he had revealed to her were sketchy. Although there was much in her husband's past they discussed rarely or not at all, she was comfortable with that.

They met in a hotel lounge on her birthday in 1977. He had wrapped a one-hundred-dollar bill around a bottle of champagne, handed it to her, and won her heart. When they married the following year, he was fun and likable and she didn't mind that he avoided talking about aspects of his former life. Several years later, he admitted to her that he had served some prison time under the name of John C. Collins. Still, she was content to allow him to talk when he wanted to or not talk if he didn't.

Now, though, her lack of reaction irritated him, even in his fragile state. Frail as he was, he managed to raise his voice loud enough that the nurses outside his room heard him nearly shout, "Oh, let it die with me!"

They sedated him then, and in eleven days, Duane was dead.

Two months later, when she sold his van, more of her husband's past was revealed. The new owner checked through the car before driving it away, found Duane's wallet in the overhead console, and turned it over to Jo. Inside the wallet were a US Navy bad conduct discharge in her husband's name, along with a prison release document from the Missouri State Penitentiary and a Social Security card in the name of "John C. Collins."

Soon after, when Jo and a good friend of hers were talking about Duane's past history, both military and criminal, Jo recalled Duane's mentioning how an old injury to his knee had come about. He said he got it jumping out of an airplane, and since she knew he spent time in the military, she accepted that—until her friend half-jokingly asked, "Did you ever think he might be D. B. Cooper?"

D. B. Cooper, the notorious skyjacker? She certainly had not. It never entered her mind, but she could hardly avoid seriously thinking about it after that conversation. She decided to investigate.

The local library had one book on D. B. Cooper. She checked it out and took it home, quite unprepared for several surprises she found in the book. The first one was the FBI's description of D. B. Cooper—mid-forties, six feet tall, 170 pounds, black hair, chain-smoker, and bourbon drinker. Her husband had been forty-seven, six-foot-one, 185 pounds, a chain-smoker, and a bourbon drinker.

And the FBI composite drawing looked very much like her dead husband. In addition, she saw several penciled notations in the book margins that she felt certain were in Duane's handwriting. One notation was the name of a town, Toutle, where a placard from the aft stairs of the 727 denoting the hazard of opening the plane's rear stairs while in flight was found in a neighboring forest by a hunter.

Oddly, in their seventeen years of marriage, Jo had never known her husband to enter the library. She decided to try to get to the bottom of this mystery.

Wasting no time, she called the FBI the same night she read the book. It was the start of a long, informal association with Ralph Himmelsbach, the agent in charge of the case from the beginning in 1971 until his retirement in 1980.

Soon, Jo learned that the notorious skyjacker had actually called himself "Dan Cooper" when he purchased his airline ticket. The name "D. B. Cooper" originated with a journalist on assignment who mistakenly recorded the skyjacker's name in his report and in that way was responsible for how Cooper has been identified ever since. As a result, the name "Dan Cooper" meant nothing to Jo when Duane tried to tell her who he really was. She so much wished she had known and was now certain he wanted her to know.

She began reading everything she could find about the only unsolved skyjacking ever carried out in the United States.

It had occurred on the day before Thanksgiving, November 24, 1971. The day was drizzly and cold, typical weather for that time of year in Oregon. Portland International Airport bustled with holiday travelers, some waiting to board Northwest Orient Airlines Flight 305 to Seattle, scheduled for a 4:35 p.m. takeoff. There were no metal detectors or pat-downs in those days. If passengers had a proper ticket and if it appeared their carry-on luggage would fit in the overhead bin, they were ushered aboard the Boeing 727-100.

Among the thirty-five passengers in the one-third-full plane was "Dan Cooper." He paid cash for a one-way ticket for the 175-mile, thirty-minute flight to the Seattle-Tacoma Airport, known as SEA-TAC in the Seattle area. Appearing to be a middle-aged executive carrying an attaché case, he wore a dark suit, loafers, a black necktie with a mother-of-pearl tie tack, and dark sunglasses. He took a seat at the rear of the cabin, where nobody was seated next to him, ordered a bourbon and water, and lit a cigarette.

At 4:45 p.m., with the pilot, Captain William W. Scott, a Northwest Orient Airlines veteran, at the controls, Flight 305 took off.

Three flight attendants were aboard: Tina Mucklow, Florence Schaffner, and the senior attendant, Alice Hancock. Florence sat nearest to Cooper for the takeoff. She was in the jump seat attached to the aft air stair door, an installation of utmost importance when Cooper chose his flight. The aft air stairs, a set of steps that can be lowered beneath the fuselage at the rear of the plane, are a feature specific to the Boeing 727. They allow passengers to board at smaller airports where the mobile ramps that attach to doorways at the forward end of a plane's sides are unavailable.

When Flight 305 was airborne, Cooper leaned toward Florence Schaffner and handed her a piece of paper. Since she was young and attractive and it had happened many times before, she assumed the note was one more traveling businessman's attempt to liven up his evening away from home. She took the note, tucked it away, and resumed looking after the other passengers. But shortly, she saw him motion to her, not in a suggestive way, but more with urgency. "Read it!" he whispered.

She did. "My God!" she said, instantly passing it to the other attendant, Tina Mucklow, who read it and had the same reaction.

The neatly printed note said the businessman had a bomb in his briefcase and wanted two-hundred thousand dollars in twenty-dollar bills and four parachutes handed over to him when they landed in Seattle. If the demands were not met, he would blow up the plane.

He indicated that Schaffner should sit in the empty seat beside him. When she did, he opened his attaché enough for her to glimpse red cylinders with wires attached, then snapped it shut again while he continued talking to her. He demanded that they land in an isolated area, that a fuel truck must be there, ready to refuel the plane, and that she should relate all this to the pilot.

Schaffner quickly made her way to the cockpit to do as she was told.

When she did, Captain Scott lost no time turning over the controls to his first officer and making his way to the back of the plane to speak with Cooper. As soon as he clearly understood the skyjacker's plans, and with the safety of his passengers uppermost in his mind, the captain radioed Cooper's exact instructions ahead to authorities on the ground.

Local police and FBI agents joined Federal Aviation Administration officers and airline and airport officials in a flurry of activity. A Seattle bank supplied the two-hundred thousand dollars in twenty-dollar bills, after they were hastily photographed—no problem there. The skyjacker's demand for nonmilitary parachutes, which give a jumper more control when the chute opens, was more difficult, but eventually the chutes were obtained.

After the plane landed safely, refueling commenced, and delivery of the money and parachutes was completed. Cooper allowed all passengers to exit the plane, leaving behind only the cockpit crew (pilot, copilot, and flight engineer) and one attendant, Tina Mucklow.

Some minor problems with an air lock during the refueling caused it to take longer than expected, which increased the war of nerves for everyone involved, but the job was finally accomplished. While that was being done, Cooper informed Captain Scott that he wanted to fly southeast toward Mexico at a specific low altitude and at a specific slow speed. Between them, they agreed that the distance would make it necessary to refuel once more later on. They settled on doing that in Reno, Nevada.

Just five people were aboard when the 727 took off at 7:40 p.m. Cooper seemed unaware of the two air force jets following them, but visibility was so poor due to the weather, and the jets flying at their slowest speed could not keep the 727 in their sights, making their value uncertain.

The businessman-turned-skyjacker ordered Mucklow to join her crewmates in the cockpit, close the door and stay there. Around 8:00 p.m., a warning light inside the cockpit flashed, indicating the aft air stair had been set in motion. Three minutes later, a significant upward movement of the plane's tail section required corrective action by the pilot. That completed, Captain Scott tried again to speak to the skyjacker over the intercom system but received no answer. There was no further communication between Cooper and the cockpit.

With the aft air stair still lowered, Captain Scott landed the 727 at 10:15 p.m. at the Reno airport, where the FBI, local police, airport police, and even army officials immediately surrounded it. Captain Scott again tried to speak with Cooper over the intercom, but there was still no answer. After several more tries, he opened the cockpit door to an empty plane. Cooper, the twenty-one-pound bundle of bills, and a parachute were gone. Cooper, it was assumed, most likely jumped when the plane's tail had noticeably jerked upward.

The mystery of D. B. Cooper and a four-state manhunt had begun.

Along with recovering as many fingerprints as they could inside the plane, the FBI picked up Cooper's tie and the tie clip he left behind. They questioned everybody who had even the slightest contact with him, gathering minute details about his appearance, speech, mannerisms—anything that might be useful. They joined the local police in rounding up suspects in the area, while the air force launched a search of the region where Cooper was presumed to have landed. The FBI even carried out an experimental flight with the same type of aircraft, reproducing the same speeds, weights, and other factors in an attempt to further pinpoint the locale where Cooper might be—dead or alive.

That the thickly forested site they focused on was a hazard to anyone jumping into it was a given, and almost everyone concluded that if the skyjacker survived, in all probability he was injured.

Some speculated that Cooper had escaped when the plane landed in Reno. The idea was that he could have crept down the aft air stairs, jumped off before the plane came to a complete stop, and fled without being seen. FBI special agent Harold E. Campbell disputed that theory, saying the airport was meticulously covered. "There's no way he could have gotten off in Reno," he said. They even had patrol boats out on some nearby lakes.

Everyone agreed that the skyjacker had done his homework. He must have known the 727 was the only commercial airliner with a door beneath the tail and with the engines positioned so that a safe jump could probably be made. Then too, Cooper must have carefully calculated the weight, the altitude, and the speed necessary for a jump to be performed without stalling the plane, since he had ordered the plane to be flown at less than ten thousand feet, with the cabin not pressurized, and at the slow speed of two hundred miles per hour with the landing gear down and flaps extended. He ordered four parachutes so they would think he might force someone to jump with him and not give him defective chutes.

Although the officials involved in the case had been painstaking in their search, Jo Weber decided to launch her own investigation. Having learned the notorious D. B. Cooper really went by the name "Dan Cooper," she recalled her husband's strange whisper to her in the hospital.

Even though FBI agent Ralph Himmelsbach, who was in charge of the case, believed the skyjacker had probably not survived his jump from the 727, he was impressed with Jo Weber's sincerity and with the fact that she never seemed interested in enriching herself from the investigation. No reward had been offered, and she wasn't interested in publicity. She cooperated with the FBI by helping to dig up witnesses simply because she wanted to know the truth about her husband.

She openly shared memories as they came back to her. One was an episode in 1978 when Duane talked in his sleep—saying something about leaving fingerprints on the aft stairs—and then woke up in a cold sweat.

Later, during a vacation, they had driven from their Florida home to the state of Washington, stopping by the Columbia River. Duane seemed to know the area well. She remembered that he walked alone near the river. Just four months later, close to that same area, an eight-year-old boy found $5,800 in deteriorated twenty-dollar bills that were never claimed.

Jo also recalled that in 1994 when she was looking over some tax papers, she came across an old Northwest Airlines plane ticket from Portland to Seattle. Duane evaded her question about it, and she couldn't find the ticket when she looked for it after he died.

Then too, in 1990, she had seen a wheat-colored canvas bag in a cooler in Duane's van. It was made of heavy, coarse material with some printing on it. The ransom money given to D. B. Cooper was in a canvas bank bag. Jo could not find the bag either after Duane died.

Shortly before his last hospitalization, he talked about the old knee injury that had happened when he jumped out of an airplane. One of the most electrifying memories she had was from that last hospitalization, when he was so very ill, sedated and semiconscious, and mumbling that he couldn't remember where he buried the bucket with $173,000 in it.

When an FBI forensic expert compared some of Jo's photos with the FBI composite of D. B. Cooper, he said, "It's about as close a match as you can get." Ralph Himmelsbach agreed. "She

D. B. Cooper FBI wanted poster

has a lot of points that stretch your imagination at the possibility of coincidence," he said.

Himmelsbach also felt that certain observations D. B. Cooper had made seemed to indicate he had served in the military, possibly had a criminal record, and definitely had some knowledge of the Oregon-Washington area. Duane had been in both the army and the navy at different times, and he had admitted to Jo that he had served time in prisons, one of which was twenty miles from the Seattle-Tacoma Airport.

As incriminating as all the evidence might appear, Duane Weber was not the only credible suspect in the skyjacking. Among more than a thousand "serious" suspects in the unsolved mystery were the usual wackos, weirdoes, publicity seekers, and wannabes, some with credible stories. A Vietnam veteran who was experienced in jump training and wilderness survival, William Gossett, confessed he was D. B. Cooper to his sons and to a friend who was a judge, but according to the FBI, there was no valid connection between him and the case.

More recently, an Oregon woman, convinced that D. B. Cooper was really her uncle, L. D. Cooper, gave the FBI a leather guitar strap belonging to her dead uncle, to check for fingerprints. If any prints are still recoverable on it, scientists will compare them to the partial ones the skyjacker left behind on the plane, recognizing that forty-year-old prints may not be entirely reliable.

Some good things did come out of the unsolved skyjacking. That it captured people's attention nationwide was underscored by the fact that in the following year, there were thirty-one more skyjackings in the United States, an unusual type of crime wave. That led to the Federal Aviation Administration (FAA) ordering all Boeing 727 planes to be fitted with an aerodynamic wedge to prevent the air stairs from being lowered while the plane was airborne. This addition is called the Cooper Vane for obvious reasons. Some airlines preferred to solve the potential problem by having the air stairs on their 727s welded shut.

Additionally in 1972, the FAA began stationing armed undercover agents on selected planes. Shortly after that, the FAA began to routinely search passengers and luggage for weapons and explosives. Another innovation inspired by the Cooper crime was the installation of peepholes in cockpit doors on most commercial aircraft. Had Flight 305 had a peephole in the cockpit door, Captain Scott and his crew might have been able to see when D. B. Cooper jumped from the plane, making it easier to pinpoint where he landed.

What confounded law experts was how D. B. Cooper became a folk hero to some people. Parties commemorated his feat, particularly in the Washington-Oregon area. The theory that Everyman challenged The Man and got away with it was a good excuse for a party, especially in Ariel, Washington, where a "D. B. Cooper Party" is held annually on the Saturday after Thanksgiving, featuring parachute jumps and a "Cooper's Corner" where copies of magazine and newspaper articles about the event are sold.

The news media descended on Ariel again in 2011 when the FBI investigated the latest tip, a supposedly credible one, concerning a Seattle man who died ten years earlier. Nothing conclusive has been determined as this book goes to print.

A romanticized movie roughly based on the real event, called *The Pursuit of D. B. Cooper,* was in movie theaters in 1981, but not for long—fortunately, according to reviewers.

Special Agent Larry Carr took over the case when Himmelsbach retired from the FBI. Carr ruled out Duane Weber as being D. B. Cooper when DNA testing became available and three skin samples on Cooper's J. C. Penney black tie left behind on the plane did not match Weber's. However, the test is in dispute since the sample consisted of just a few cells and was highly susceptible to contamination.

The case is still open, but Carr thinks chances are remote that Cooper survived.

"Diving into the wilderness without the right equipment, in such terrible conditions, he probably never even got his chute open," he said.

CHAPTER 10

Search for Amy

March 5, 1974, in Coconut Grove was another perfect Florida day—blue skies, warm sunshine, with a gentle breeze off Biscayne Bay. Crowds strolled along the brick sidewalks, stopping to browse at the quaint shops or snack at the sidewalk cafes.

Seventeen-year-old Amy Billig came home from school minutes after Sue, her mother, and a friend had left the house for a few hours at the beach. Amy snacked on yogurt while she phoned Ned, her father, asking to borrow two dollars for lunch she wanted to have with girlfriends in Peacock Park. He agreed, so she headed for his Dimensions Art Gallery, an easy walk, less than a mile, on the bustling streets. She waved as always to construction workers building a house in the neighborhood, and they waved back.

Amy was never seen again.

When she wasn't home for dinner, her mother started to worry. Amy and her younger brother, Josh, were never late.

Ned said Amy hadn't come for the money. Her girlfriends soon called, wondering why she had not shown up at the park.

That was enough for Sue. She phoned a family friend, Mike Gonzalez, a detective and himself the father of teenagers, who came right over. From experience, Gonzalez knew most missing teens returned safely without assistance. He reassured the family, adding that if Amy hadn't returned by morning, they should call him again.

Sue did call him at 6:00 a.m., beginning a search that would continue far into the future.

No one in the Billig family was a native Floridian. Sue was a jazz singer and Ned a jazz trumpet player when they lived in New York City. Married ten years before Amy came along after Sue's four miscarriages, they considered her their miracle baby. The following year, they were blessed with the birth of a son, Joshua.

Wanting the best for their family, Sue and Ned worried about the violence in New York City at that time. So in 1969, Coconut Grove, a historic residential community south of Miami with lush green streets, a vibrant arts district, and quiet neighborhoods, became their home.

Ned opened an art gallery while Sue found work in interior design. With a home in a charming community, a 1954 Bentley in the driveway, their children doing well in private schools, life was good. Until March 5, 1974.

From the start, Sue was unhappy with the lack of attention the local police gave Amy's disappearance. Six days passed before the story was finally reported in the news media. Friends and neighbors, who immediately set up a fund at the Coconut Grove Bank to pay for search expenses, appeared more proactive than the authorities.

Ned worked exhaustively with a private detective while Sue handed out fliers and tacked up posters with Amy's photo. Josh and his friends searched streets where he and his sister used to walk. As the tips and leads poured in, each of them first aroused the family's hopes, then dashed them to the ground when none amounted to anything.

After nearly two weeks, a young woman phoned, refusing to be identified, but stating positively that she saw the biker gang, known as the Outlaws, kidnap Amy off the street. The day Amy disappeared, scores of bikers had brazenly thundered through the Grove, riding five abreast on their way north to races in Daytona Beach.

Amy enjoyed hitchhiking through the neighborhood, with neighbors, not bikers. But she was so open and guileless, their sweet, 102-pound, poetry-writing, musically talented, animal-loving vegetarian. Surely she wouldn't . . . At the time, the issue of missing children was not as highly publicized as it became later. Amy was so trusting that it was hard to know what to think.

A few days later, a Billig acquaintance who was a bail bondsman arranged a meeting between them and two Outlaws. The bikers' appearance was off-putting—dirty jeans, switchblades protruding from back pockets, black jackets with the Outlaw insignia across their backs, muddy steel-toed boots—but they pledged their help, the first really encouraging thing that happened. Hopes were soon diminished, however, when the bikers phoned a few days later, telling the Billigs to drop it, because nothing could be done. Drop it, they said. Their final words.

It would not be the last time Sue, Ned, and Josh would dare to hope, only to endure crushing disappointment.

On March 18, another clue surfaced with a tie-in to bikers. Amy's camera was found beside an off-ramp of the Florida Turnpike near Orlando, the logical route for bikers on the way north to Daytona. The Billig family had no idea when Amy last used her camera, whether she might have tossed it there as a clue, or if it had previously been stolen, or any other reason why the camera was found where it was. The young man who found it delivered it to the Billigs' home, but when they developed the film inside, only one photo was not overexposed, and it showed an unremarkable vine-covered building and a white truck, totally unfamiliar.

Two days later, the phone call they had been waiting for came through. Sue answered and heard a feeble female-sounding voice in the background crying, "Mama, Mama, please help—" Amy? Was it her? Alive! Sue couldn't be sure, but her hands shook, her heart raced.

A young male voice gave Sue explicit instructions. She was ordered to dress in red, white, and blue, carry a black briefcase with thirty thousand dollars in small bills inside, and bring it to the lobby of the Fontainebleau Hotel at 11:00 a.m. She must come alone or Amy would be killed.

Sue tried to stay calm, clinging fiercely to Ned before they began forming a plan.

It took some doing, but a sympathetic friend, a bank president, arranged to supply the money in marked bills. No one they knew had a black briefcase, so they painted one black. The FBI was notified, and plainclothes police officers would mingle among the Fontainebleau guests.

Sue was sure no one else could be as shaky as she was while she and an undercover policewoman, posing as her good friend, waited in the busy hotel lobby. Soon, a young man with a bad complexion and a ponytail under his green baseball cap approached. He obviously was a close second in the nerves department.

When he demanded to know why she hadn't come alone, Sue said she recently moved from New York City and didn't know how to drive.

He accepted that. His youth and nervousness relieved Sue enough that she refused to give him the briefcase until he showed proof he had Amy.

Consequently, he led the two women to the fifth floor, where the police, responding to hand signals from the plainclothes policewoman with Sue, were waiting. They arrested the boy and his twin brother, who was the one who cried out, "Mama, Mama," over the phone. Sue was certain she felt her heart break.

The boys, who were from a well-to-do family, showed no remorse for their cruel farce—not even when Sue refused to press charges. Because of her kindness, the boys were released into their divorced mother's custody, facing no jail time. Sue and Ned were satisfied that the boys were not punished further, and they even accepted not being reimbursed by the boys' family for expenses incurred from their sons' stupidity. They did resent the boys for showing no hint of repentance, and, more importantly, for having diverted attention from legitimate leads.

As for Sue and Ned and Josh, their tortured days continued as they hoped, waited, and prayed that the next phone call or letter would be the one they hoped for. Someone, usually Sue, stayed near the telephone, praying for the one phone call that would lead them to finding Amy.

There were false leads, calls from psychics telling them where to find her and some from people offering prayers. Sue recorded every phone conversation on tape and in notebooks kept beside each telephone in the house. When she could stand the tension no longer, she left the phone to someone else and passed out fliers with Amy's picture at traffic intersections.

Ned forced himself to attend Amy's graduation from high school in absentia, expressing the family's gratitude to her classmates who raised over $1,500 for the Amy Fund.

Josh, formerly an outgoing boy, retreated into himself, sparing his parents the pain he endured listening to the hateful taunts from some classmates who claimed they had his sister tied up in their room or worse.

In time, an old friend from Baltimore called, saying his lawyer worked with bikers, and some of them told him they had taken a girl from Miami when they were headed to the races at Daytona. The friend phoned a second time, saying gang members reported the Outlaws had Amy when they left Fort Lauderdale. The Outlaws again.

Amy Billig memorial

Every call was investigated. In June, one came from a Treasury Department worker, certain she had seen Amy with rowdy bikers, looking "spaced out" in a Fort Lauderdale bar. Sue sped to Fort Lauderdale, located the bar and its owner, who remembered the group and knew the bikers were Outlaws from Orlando.

What was another two hundred miles? Or another search? Sue hopped in the car, sped to follow skimpy leads on Outlaws in Orlando and nearby Kissimmee. She eventually uncovered what she considered a real clue at a Majik Market. The manager recalled a girl fitting Amy's description coming in occasionally with two bikers. He remembered the girl always bought crackers and Campbell's Vegetarian Vegetable soup. Amy, their vegetarian daughter?

Sue located the Outlaw clubhouse without much trouble. It was empty and filthy, but she gritted her teeth, forced herself to enter, took photos, and searched. The garbage yielded a phone bill with one frequently called number. Sue pocketed it along with some hairs she pulled from a discarded hairbrush, before she drove back to Miami, where bad news awaited.

After five months, the police finally answered her plea to come to their home to take Amy's fingerprints from her bedroom. Too late. Florida's humidity is hard on fingerprints, and none that could be used were left in Amy's bedroom after so much time had passed. Why, oh why hadn't they come when she asked them to?

They tested hairs in Amy's brush. In comparing them to the ones Sue brought back from Orlando, the results showed they could be a match but were inconclusive.

One call among many that kept coming to the Billigs' home was from a sympathetic biker who told Sue that an Outlaw he knew swore Amy had been sold in Fort Lauderdale when a number of bikers were rounded up and jailed. That was all Sue needed. She sped to the Raiford and the Belle Glade prisons to learn what she could from incarcerated bikers.

What she learned was that bikers are like fraternity brothers in that they will not talk about each other. Although some of them claimed to have seen Amy with other bikers, the trips to the prisons were ultimately a wasted effort.

It was becoming increasingly hard for the Billig family to trust people, even some who seemed decent and conscientious. Two ex-policemen convinced Sue and Ned that they could bring Amy back but would need three thousand dollars for expenses. The Bentley had been sold, much of Sue's jewelry was sold;

finances were getting tight. All Ned could raise was $1,500, which the men agreed would be enough to start. They promised to keep in touch but made no phone calls until much later, when they only reported they could not find Amy.

A year had passed since Amy had disappeared. Frustrated, Sue again took things into her own hands. Using the phone number she found on the bill in the Outlaw clubhouse in Orlando, she telephoned the president of the Florida Outlaws, appropriately named Big Jim. It took a lot of talking, but by then she was getting good at that. He grudgingly agreed to meet her at his place in Hollywood, twenty-five miles away.

His house was about what she expected—rusted car parts were scattered over the dirt lawn; the inside was filthy and smelled of marijuana. A few huge, stone-faced bikers, obviously spaced out, lounged on bare mattresses. Only the possibility of finding a clue concerning Amy kept Sue from running out the door.

She gingerly sipped at the beer can Big Jim insisted she have while he questioned her. Gradually, he seemed convinced she wouldn't have the law after him. He agreed to ask around, try to find some answers. He would call her home.

Time passed with no calls from him. Upon investigating, the Billigs learned he was in jail for assaulting a policeman. Next, they heard he had been indicted for the murder of three Hell's Angels. There would be no help from Big Jim for some time.

It seemed any news of Amy would be better than none when a biker named Paul phoned. He saw a story about Amy in the newspaper and was sure he had "owned" her before he was arrested. His description of her was so accurate that Sue agreed to meet him at an out-of-the-way gas station.

He was huge, hairy, tattooed, and smelled bad, but she pushed aside her fear and climbed on the back of his motorcycle to ride to his trailer. Once there, Paul studied Sue's photos of Amy, becoming even more certain it was Amy he'd had and loved before his arrest. He learned from other bikers that she was now in Tulsa.

He promised to meet Sue there. They would find Amy. Sue wondered: Could the ordeal really be coming to an end?

She flew to Tulsa, got a room at a hotel, and waited for Paul. And waited. For five weeks she waited, showing Amy's picture wherever she thought it might help. Finally she flew home, empty, sad, defeated.

There was so little she could do. She did what she could, wrote letters, passed out fliers, prayed.

Paul finally did call one night at 4:00 a.m., opening the conversation with a surly explanation that his kneecaps were broken. Amy, he said, was working in Seattle, dancing in some dive. This, Paul added, would be the last time Sue would ever hear from him.

She immediately started making preparations for a trip to Seattle, trying to ignore some strange sensations in her chest. The feeling quickly changed from strange to frighteningly painful. Over her protests, Ned hustled her to Jackson Memorial Hospital, where she was admitted to the cardiac intensive care unit, arguing that she *couldn't* have heart disease. Still protesting, she underwent bypass surgery.

In a remarkably short time after her operation, the indomitable mother flew to Seattle. She checked in at the police headquarters, where the police informed her there were no bikers in Seattle.

No longer a beginner, Sue searched and found some Outlaws on her own. She explained herself to them, showed Amy's photo, asked for their help. She always assured bikers she wasn't looking to have anyone arrested but only wanted her daughter back. She won them over. Convinced of her sincerity, they made an earnest effort to find Amy, but it was another dead end.

To show her gratitude for their help, she accepted their invitation to have Thanksgiving dinner with them before flying back to Florida.

Four years had gone by since Amy disappeared. Four years of false leads, adrenaline rushes, crushing heartbreaks. Sue continued to take as many interior design assignments as she could to earn money, but Ned had to close his gallery and take a manager's job in another store. They lost their home and moved to a smaller one. Both constantly worried that they had been neglecting Josh, but the search had to continue. No possible lead was ever passed over without a thorough vetting.

Amy had been gone five years when Edna Buchanan, the *Miami Herald* police reporter, published a story about Amy in *Tropic*, the Sunday magazine section. As expected, phone calls, letters, tips, and prayers flooded in. Along with all the kindness, there were a few less desirable phone calls, including one from a man claiming to be Hal Johnson from Fort Pierce. He said that he had seen the article and saw a girl who looked like Amy teamed up with bikers. He agreed to meet the Billigs to look at more pictures.

The three arranged to meet, but the polite man did not appear. Days later, he phoned again, apologizing profusely and offering Sue and Ned the opportunity to see the girl themselves. He gave them a Fort Pierce phone number and address where the girl would be posing for him and another artist.

Trying not to get too excited, Sue called the number just to check and was not surprised to hear a recording saying the number was out of service. She phoned the Fort Pierce police, who investigated, then returned her call saying there was no such address.

Unfortunately, it would not be the last of Hal Johnson's calls. He called as often as six or seven times a day, even at 4:00 a.m., and the calls became increasingly revolting, insulting, and vicious. When Ned answered, Johnson would hang up. It was Sue he wanted to torture. And he did, for seventeen years.

Even if it might deter Johnson for a time, there was no way Sue would change the phone number. It was the only number Amy knew.

Sue felt she needed to alert her old neighbors to keep watch in case Amy came back to their old house, but when she returned there, she saw to her dismay that the former Billig home was being demolished to make way for a new one. There was nothing to do but cry a bit and then beg old neighbors to keep watch for Amy.

Life was taking its toll on the Billig family. Ned sank into a deep depression, frequently resorting to alcohol to dull his pain, which in turn caused tension between him and Josh. When Josh married in 1988, he and his wife had a daughter who bore an uncanny resemblance to her missing aunt. Ned and Sue doted on their granddaughter but often felt a searing pain when they looked at her.

Another catastrophe struck in 1992, when Sue, a non-smoker, developed cancer in both lungs. Following surgery and chemotherapy, she swore, "I will not die until I find Amy."

Hal Johnson continued his vicious calls, even when Sue told him she was diagnosed with lung cancer, hoping that it would touch some bit of humanity in him. But it made no difference.

Incredibly, as Sue began to feel a bit better, Ned, a heavy smoker, was also diagnosed with lung cancer. He passed on quickly.

Hal Johnson waited just two weeks after Ned's obituary was published before resuming his filthy, hateful calls.

Now, however, improved technology was on the law's side. Johnson had been using a cell phone, originally difficult to trace. With the FBI's help, the calls were finally traced to a specific number. FBI agents called the number, astounded to hear US Customs answer.

Hal Johnson, they learned, was Henry Johnson Blair, a highly decorated customs agent. He denied being the man they were looking for until confronted with incontrovertible evidence. Even when there was no way out, he blamed his despicable behavior on an "obsessive-compulsive thing," showing no remorse for the woman who was dealing with her own cancer, the death of her beloved husband, and twenty-two excruciatingly painful years of searching for her missing daughter.

Blair was sentenced to two years in prison for aggravated stalking, with five years' probation and counseling.

Sue was not permitted in the courtroom during Blair's testimony. Until the trial was over, she hadn't heard his words about her: "She's not as innocent as she seems. Did she ever take a lie detector polygraph? It occurred to me, she could have buried the kid in the backyard."

That did it. Sue brought suit against Blair, winning a civil lawsuit for five million dollars against her tormentor. Due to his financial situation, she had to settle for Blair paying her six thousand to seven thousand dollars a year.

Sue suffered three more heart attacks but never stopped looking for her daughter.

She died in 2005 from complications of heart disease—or more likely a broken heart.

The mystery of Amy's disappearance has never been solved.

CHAPTER 11

Florida's Own Captain Midnight

I t was just past midnight on Sunday, April 27, 1986. Home
Box Office viewers were following an espionage movie, *The
Falcon and the Snowman,* starring Timothy Hutton and Sean
Penn. Suddenly, for viewers in the Eastern Time Zone, the pic-
ture and sound were interrupted by a color bar test pattern filling
the screen. Then in an instant, a message appeared over the bar:

"GOODEVENING HBO

FROM CAPTAIN MIDNIGHT

$12.95/MONTH?

NO WAY!

(SHOWTIME/MOVIE CHANNEL BEWARE)"

At the HBO studio on Long Island, New York, the usually
calm engineers on duty turned frantic, struggling to override the
alien signal. Every time they managed to restore the signal for a
few seconds, Captain Midnight increased his power, too, and his

message filled the screen again. The two signals took turns over-powering each other every sixty to ninety seconds, until, after four and a half minutes, Captain Midnight left the premises and John MacDougall, model citizen, returned.

MacDougall was a resident of Ocala, Florida, a quiet, family-oriented community in the center of the state. Until then, the only law he had ever broken was driving over the fifty-five mile per hour speed limit.

At the dawn of 1986, the future looked bright for twenty-five-year-old MacDougall. He had started and owned a successful satellite dealership business, MacDougall Electronics, in Ocala, a small city that boasts an impressive historical district and is surrounded by picturesque horse farms. The Ocala National Forest and the Silver Springs are nearby. Orlando's theme parks and other attractions and the beaches of both coasts can be reached within an hour. A great place to live, a promising business—all in all, the new year looked bright.

Then, two weeks into January, Home Box Office launched what at first seemed an insignificant action, but one that eventually became described as a 1986 version of *Star Wars*. On January 15, HBO scrambled its signal full time, around the clock, resulting in unwatchable images and preventing dish owners from viewing television programs unless they paid HBO's monthly fees. The Movie Channel and Showtime promised to begin scrambling on May 27, to be followed shortly by ESPN, MTV, and others before the year was out. The owners of the approximately 1.5 million homes that depended on direct satellite reception were incensed.

The jilted customers demanded to know why programs sent over public airwaves weren't free to anyone who had the gear to pick them up, as it was with network television and radio. Why should farmers and their neighbors have to pay a fee every month, especially since they had already paid two thousand to five thousand dollars to buy a dish in the first place? Now they were expected to pay for a descrambler at a cost of about $395 as well as a monthly program fee similar to that paid by cable subscribers—$12.95 for HBO and $10.95 for Showtime. Not fair, they grumbled.

Back in 1979, when dishes first became available to homeowners, many rural residents whose homes were located beyond the limits of cable connection were elated to be able to view television programs for the first time ever. They could point their dishlike antenna to one of several satellites orbiting the Earth and view not only prominent entertainment channels, but even foreign programs and some private transmissions of network programs, all unedited and without commercials.

The dishes originally sold for ten thousand dollars, but as prices dropped, the news about them circulated and more people switched. Sales spread from the farms to cities and suburbs, drastically cutting into the cable business.

Not surprisingly, after HBO scrambled its signal, dish sales dropped from about seventy thousand a month in the fall of

1985 to less than fifteen thousand in January 1986. Ten dealers in one suburb went out of business within two weeks. MacDougall Electronics had done well since its opening, but the sudden widespread drop in sales seemed a bad omen. MacDougall economized wherever he could, but bills still had to be paid while he waited for the customers who never came.

To help pay his bills, he took a swing-shift job as a part-time engineer at a satellite transmission company, Central Florida Teleport. He was a natural at it. From a young age, he liked to tinker—radios, cars, whatever.

On Saturday, April 26, MacDougall had what had become a typical day for him. He read magazines in his empty shop while waiting for nonexistent customers. He could hardly have helped thinking about why his once bright future appeared to be going down the tubes. Why should he, an honest, hard-working businessman, have to watch his great American dream fade away because of some greedy big businesses?

He closed MacDougall Electronics at 4:00 p.m. that afternoon, picked up a sandwich for his dinner later on, and went to his second job at Central Florida Teleport, which was in a small building, made to look even smaller by the five huge satellite dishes installed beside it outdoors. One other engineer was on duty with him until 6:00 p.m., and then MacDougall was left to run the operation on his own. With his skills, it was an easy job.

He fended off boredom by keeping an eye on the evening's program, *Pee-Wee's Big Adventure*, a forgettable movie presented over the airwaves by the now defunct pay-per-view People's Choice network.

When the movie and his shift ended, he followed his normal routine, swinging the teleport's thirty-foot dish back to its regular downtime position. This was necessary to protect the dish in case of rain, which could cause it to dislodge in the unstable soil beneath it. When in place, MacDougall knew the dish was aimed directly at Galaxy I and at the exact point, Transponder 23, that carried HBO.

That was the moment when he made his decision. There was no stopping to ponder the right or wrong of it, whether he should or should not do it, or what the consequences might be. It came to him that he could do something about the unfairness of the battle between the big guys and the regular guys—something he was in a unique position to do. He quickly worked a message out in his head, wanting to keep it simple and polite, with no name-calling.

He had recently seen a low-budget movie, *On the Air Live with Captain Midnight,* about a teenage technical nerd who became a success using a powerful CB radio to run a rolling pirate radio station. *Hmmm,* MacDougall thought. *Captain Midnight.*

He knew which button to push to transmit a color bar pattern, and at 12:32 a.m. on April 27, he pushed it. With one movement of his finger on the transmit button, the former law-abiding citizen became an unseen mythical hero to the country's more than 1.5 million home satellite dish owners. His identity was a mystery, but he was their hero.

However, along with Captain Midnight, guilt also entered the scene. John's out-of-character actions began troubling him immediately as he went about the business of setting the teleport's equipment back to normal. Feelings of guilt nagged at him most of that night. The next morning, he was surprised to find that news of his exploit had been picked up and broadcast on network television.

The rest of the world wanted to know—who was Captain Midnight? Was he a hero or a villain?

The original Captain Midnight, a comic book character of the 1940s, was definitely a mythical hero, a World War II pilot who always returned from his dangerous missions at midnight. Certainly the real-life hero of the 1986 adventure of Captain Midnight was a mystery, but the reverberations of his doings had already begun.

It was considered a daring bit of a monkeyshine by some, but HBO didn't see it that way. What it was was another broadside fired between the cable television programmers and the satellite dish business that could have far-reaching and serious consequences.

Authorities with the Federal Communications Commission (FCC) immediately launched an intensive investigation to ferret out the mysterious Captain Midnight. Clearly, they were worried. One spokesman said, "We will prosecute with whatever resources we have."

COURTESY OF JOHN MACDOUGALL

John MacDougall

David Pritchard, vice president of HBO, proclaimed the incident "a criminal, willful interference of a government-licensed satellite broadcast." His firm had already received many threats of interruptions to its services after its plans were announced. This could only worsen the situation.

HBO was in the forefront, but other cable programmers also worried that with all the publicity, Captain Midnight might turn into a folk hero of enormous proportions. HBO would obviously be the designated villain.

The highly publicized case of deliberate interference with a satellite transmission attracted attention in many quarters. Karl Savatiel, the director of satellite communications for AT&T, stated, "Most satellites are built with some safety measures. But all satellites, including military satellites, are vulnerable if a person knows where the satellite is located, the frequency it uses for transmission, and the sender's code."

William Russell, speaking for the FCC, pronounced the interference a violation of the Communications Act, possibly entailing a ten-thousand-dollar fine and a year in prison. The Justice Department also showed signs of getting involved. Additionally, the House Communications Subcommittee planned to hold hearings on the subject of satellite jamming.

Other congressional representatives were showing interest, too. Those from states with extensive rural areas were more sympathetic to satellite dish owners. Comprising mostly farmers and their families, those folks already felt disrespected by the big city powers and were looking for some consideration.

Senator Dale Bumpers of Arkansas offered that, because dish owners put out so much money for a dish, they had the right to receive signals at a reasonably equitable cost, just as people in cities could receive them with cable service. Senators

Timothy Wirth of Colorado, Nancy Kassebaum of Kansas, Wendell Ford of Kentucky, and Barry Goldwater of Arizona all agreed.

HBO's fears about Captain Midnight becoming a folk hero were turning out to be justified. His daring action made headlines, became *the* topic around the office watercooler, and was even discussed on the popular Johnny Carson television show. The cable television industry collectively shuddered.

The FCC assigned an agent, George Dillon, to the case. Dillon was convinced that the incident involved a threat to national security. He was concerned that copycat incidents could disrupt "things like defense, communications, medical information, telephone communication, and teleconferences." Inevitably, the question came up—could Captain Midnight be a terrorist?

In Ocala, Florida, John R. MacDougall began his day with the uncomfortable realization that the repercussions of his actions were under way.

Satellite station operators were forced to recognize the frailty of their service. The FCC chairman pushed for the commission to capture Captain Midnight. Other HBO representatives admitted they had received numerous threats of foul-ups if they continued with the signal scrambling. At their urging, the FCC swung into action.

Since home dishes can only receive signals, not send them, investigators assumed the overpowering signal must have

originated at a site with a large dish—thirty to forty feet wide—
a strong transmitter, at least four thousand watts of power, and
a higher antenna than those found in most homes. That alone
narrowed the search considerably. There were still 580 uplink
facilities with large enough dishes to be possibilities, but by
scrupulously studying the tapes made of the transmission, the
FCC sleuths were able to identify the type of electronic character generator Captain Midnight had used, which narrowed the
investigation down to one hundred locations that owned that
type of equipment.

The FCC determined the particular time HBO's signal
was overpowered, and Central Florida Teleport was the only
facility with the necessary equipment that could have been used
to write the message at that time. Additionally, in the week
before the message appeared, HBO programming had been
briefly obstructed with a pattern of color bars at the same time,
indicating the same person at the same place at the same time.
(MacDougall reportedly admitted to this at one time, but denied
it at another.)

In the meantime, further checking showed that MacDougall was the only one working at Central Florida Teleport at both
times in question. So it was that John R. MacDougall, the five-
foot-eleven, 225-pound conscientious taxpayer who claimed that
he had never even purchased a beer before the legal age limit,
and who still believed he had done a good thing, was arrested,
photographed, and fingerprinted.

Three months of intensive detective work by FCC agents had paid off. MacDougall, informed that he had a 70 percent chance of winning his case, but that he could be fined one hundred thousand dollars and face the possibility of a year in jail if he lost, pleaded guilty at his hearing in July. In August, he was relieved to be sentenced to pay a fine of five thousand dollars, serve one year's probation, and have his radio operator's license suspended, rather than the much harsher sentence he could have received. True to form, Citizen MacDougall claimed he was always treated with respect by all authorities at all times.

He returned to his life in Ocala where the FCC's concerns about him becoming a folk hero were realized. Dish owners and satellite TV dealers were grateful to him for the publicity he brought to their cause. A group formed, calling itself the Captain Midnight Grassroots Coalition; it sold T-shirts and bumper stickers to help MacDougall with his legal costs. His peaceful, nonconfrontational method of protesting the deeds of the big and the powerful appealed to the group's members.

The media had been closely following the case, and when they learned the authorities got their man, there was no holding them back. In hordes, they descended on Ocala, where suddenly Ocala's model citizen was front-page news. MacDougall's life turned difficult in a decidedly different way from what it had been before April 27.

He found the publicity especially hard to live with, what with reporters and photographers constantly following him, plus the inescapable, never-ending phone calls. It would be the biggest problem he had to deal with—that and his family's embarrassment. With passing time, however, his family came around and actually took pride in how he had taken a stand for something he truly believed needed to be done, particularly since it wasn't done only for himself.

Questioned later by this writer, MacDougall said he really had no regrets about the matter, except that at the time, he had no idea how big a deal it would be in the media. "If I had known," he said, "I would have taken steps to not get caught."

The frustrations with cable television services inspired more than this one instance of rebellion. Earlier, the Disney Channel briefly had its programming overridden by an off-color signal; later, in 1987, a hacker broke into a Chicago superstation broadcast of a British science fiction series wearing a Max Headroom mask. This trespasser dropped his pants to moon the viewers and was swatted on his bare bottom by a flyswatter held by someone off camera.

That same year, an engineer at the Christian Broadcasting Network (CBN) interrupted two soft-porn channels with religious messages. The defendant, Thomas Haynie, supported by Pat Robertson, was the first person convicted of satellite piracy, a felony. Haynie was put on probation, fined, and required to perform community service. He was also dismissed from his job at CBN.

Although MacDougall took his Captain Midnight name from the movie *On the Air Live with Captain Midnight,* the original Captain Midnight was a comic book character in the 1940s, a radio series later on, and a television series in the 1950s. A new book, *The Captain Midnight Chronicles,* has stories featuring a blend of all versions of the character and is still selling well.

However, the myth never seemed to fade, which MacDougall has realized on more than one occasion, such as when he learned that the story of Captain Midnight—his story—was a topic of discussion in a graduate journalism class at a university in Hawaii. Another time, he took a phone call from his niece, who told him how surprised she was when she played a game of Trivial Pursuit with friends and a question came up about Captain Midnight—his version again.

Ever a man of honor, MacDougall looked after both parents until his father died in 2009, and he has continued looking after his elderly mother whose condition requires close supervision. After twenty years in his original business, he is now semi-retired but still owns MacDougall Electronics, which continues to sell and install satellite dishes.

In 2011, the twenty-fifth anniversary of Captain Midnight's satellite message, MacDougall maintains that he has no regrets about trying to get his message out "to corporate America about unfair pricing and restrictive trade practices."

CHAPTER 12

The Dark Side of the Sunshine Skyway Bridge

The uncluttered lines of the majestic Sunshine Skyway Bridge soar over the open waters of Tampa Bay, drawing tourists, reporters from travel magazines, photographers filming car commercials, and people intent on ending their lives.

The original two-lane bridge was built in 1954. Then, to provide for the ever-increasing vehicular traffic, a second matching span was opened in 1971 west of the first one, with northbound traffic traveling on the original span and southbound traffic on the newer one. Traffic beneath the bridge increased, too, and after several ships hit and caused structural damage to bridge supports, an entirely new bridge was built and opened in 1987.

The initial structure is rumored to have been built over a Tocobaga burial mound, a sacred area to the extinct tribe of Native Americans. They believed a curse would torment anyone who violated sacred burial plots. Could that curse have continued on, protecting the spirits of the dead by following the parallel structure that was built alongside the original one to remake it into a four-lane bridge? The subsequent tragic accidents, suicides, ghost sightings, and at least one murder-suicide suggest that the ancient curse persists today.

From its earliest days, the bridge proved a popular attraction for those depressed enough to want to end their lives. Precise numbers cannot be confirmed because it was not always possible to recover bodies, but barely five months after the new bridge opened in 1987, the first person leaped to his death from it. From that time on, at least 135 people have jumped from the center span of the Sunshine Skyway Bridge.

Soon after the original bridge opened in 1954, a maid ended her life there, though her husband desperately tried to restrain her, clutching at her clothing and pleading with her not to leave him.

A bookkeeper who plunged to his death in 1963 left behind a book of poems in his car. Possibly to explain his action, he had marked one poem, his message to the world he left behind. It read:

> *I am standing on the threshold of eternity at last,*
> *As reckless of the future as I have been of the past:*
> *I am void of all ambition, I am dead of every hope:*
> *The coil of life is ended; I am letting go the rope.*
>
> —Author unknown

Tragically, a few unfortunate souls were actually forced against their will into Tampa Bay's beautiful waters, but on the other hand, at least thirty would-be jumpers became survivors, having been deterred in one way or another.

One troubled young man, despondent over his divorce, observed the holiday on July 4, 1992, by fastening a rope to his car bumper, the other end around his neck, and then hanging himself from the top of the northbound bridge span. Before the highway patrol officer on duty could reach him, the young man became the first person to do himself in by hanging from the bridge.

The following year, two teenagers who were in love and facing separation because the boy's family was about to move away took a cab to the bridge on a lovely August evening. The girl's mother, alarmed when her punctual daughter was not home by 11:00 p.m., contacted a friend, who recalled the girl mentioning something about the Sunshine Skyway Bridge. Investigators found both teenagers' names written on the bridge concrete in lipstick in the girl's favorite shade. A Coast Guard patrol boat recovered the sixteen-year-old girl's body the next day in the water just west of the bridge. Both of her legs had broken in the fall. The following day, the boyfriend's battered, lifeless body was fished from the water when a tugboat crew spotted it.

Although each of these incidents represents an individual tragedy, 1980 proved to be a deadly year for the Sunshine Skyway Bridge curse. In near perfect weather on January 28, around 8:24 p.m., the US Coast Guard buoy tender *Blackthorn* was leaving Tampa to return to her home port in Galveston, Texas, after undergoing a four-month overhaul.

Ships from all over the world enter and leave Tampa Bay, the nation's seventh busiest port, at all hours of the day and night. The channel from the Gulf of Mexico to the port of Tampa is forty-three miles long, one of the longest in the world, with eight inbound turns and twelve outbound turns. In a few places it is too narrow for big ships to pass each other.

There was little room for maneuvering the 180-foot *Blackthorn* as the incoming 605-foot tanker *Capricorn* approached, both vessels proceeding at full speed. When they collided about one mile from the Sunshine Skyway Bridge, the *Blackthorn* became entangled in *Capricorn's* anchor chain. The fortunate *Capricorn* was undamaged, but after her anchor ripped the *Blackthorn* hull open, that ship capsized and sank within ten minutes.

Although injured, some *Blackthorn* crew members were able to make their way through the submerged compartments, escaping into icy waters that reeked of diesel fuel. Fishermen in nearby boats assisted in rescuing them.

The lights of the bridge twinkled down on twenty-three men who perished in the worst peacetime loss of life in Coast Guard history. Their names are inscribed on a tablet in a memorial park at the north end of the bridge.

Salvage operations on the *Blackthorn* were completed and normal commerce in the bay resumed within a few weeks, but just four months later, the bridge was the scene of another horrific disaster. This second disaster further cemented some Floridians' belief that the curse of the Sunshine Skyway Bridge remained a force to be respected.

Tampa Bay's long channel and shallow water by themselves can be treacherous to ships, but the 4.1-mile bridge was built to connect the shortest distance between two points, positioning the ship channel diagonally beneath it, which further complicates piloting huge vessels through. As a result, the channel beneath the bridge is considered one of the most hazardous in the world.

Around 7:30 a.m. on May 9, in a driving rain, sudden tropical storm winds that had not been forecast, fog, and near zero visibility, the bow of the *Summit Venture,* a 608-foot-long freighter, slammed into pier 2S of the Sunshine Skyway Bridge. Within seconds, 1,200 feet of the bridge crashed into the bay and with it, six cars, a pickup truck, and a bus. Some thirty-five terrified human beings lived the last few moments of their lives hurtling 150 feet to their deaths.

Amazingly, the driver of the pickup truck survived. His truck landed on top of the ship before it bounced off and tumbled into the bay, but he managed to get out and was picked up by a rescue boat. The Greyhound bus, now sometimes called the "ghost bus," was so severely damaged that the top sheared off and the driver and all twenty-six passengers sank into watery graves. Autopsies on the recovered bodies proved that almost all died from impact injuries. A few drowned, but they, too, had such severe impact injuries that they would have been unconscious before they drowned.

The accident is labeled one of the worst bridge disasters in the nation's history.

The sad episode was not yet finished. The demolished Greyhound bus that was crossing the bridge at the time of the catastrophe was fished out of the bay, its undamaged parts used to repair other buses. It has since been reported that nearly all of the repaired buses have subsequently burst into flames for no apparent reason.

During the fifteen days it took to recover the bodies and clear the channel of the wrecked vehicles and other debris, the northbound side of the bridge became one lane in each direction for vehicular traffic. It remained that way until the new bridge opened.

With its golden sail-like appearance, the new bridge is 50 percent wider, nearly fifty feet higher at the center for large ships to pass, and able to withstand stronger winds. Its pilings are protected by mounds of boulders and surrounded by bumpers called dolphins. Both approaches from the old bridge were turned into the Skyway Fishing Pier State Park.

The image of the ill-fated bus persists in occasional reports of a phantom Greyhound bus motoring along the present-day fishing pier. The driver is said to stare straight ahead until the bus disappears off the pier, leaving behind a faint scent of gas fumes. Some who reported seeing the bus swore that a woman dressed in black smiled and waved from the rear window as the bus passed by.

It would not be the last "bus story" connected to the magnificent bridge. In 2004, a charter bus used as a shuttle by Amtrak nearly suffered the same fate as the Greyhound, but this time, there was a happier ending. Just as the bus, with five passengers, neared the top of the bridge, the driver slumped over, crumpled in a heap by the doors. Three passengers rushed to the front of the bus as it bounced and scraped against the concrete safety barrier.

Two women grabbed the steering wheel, while one woman's husband slid into the driver's seat, frantically trying to keep the bus from crashing into other lanes of speeding traffic as he searched for, then slammed on the brake. The passengers were uninjured, but terrified, speechless, and short of breath. Rescue crews took the driver to the hospital where he died later, probably from a second heart attack. So, while the unfortunate episode had a better ending than many tales connected to the bridge, one life was lost and it, too, must be counted as part of the Sunshine Skyway history.

Many stories in the history of the bridge involve young women, some blond, some dressed in white. As early as the 1960s, several drivers crossing the bridge described seeing a blond-haired woman dressed in white, positioned as if ready to jump from the center of the bridge. Sightings of her were particularly common if the area was foggy, but when authorities investigated, no woman was ever found. More than once, another fair-haired young woman, this one in bare feet, was reported to be hitchhiking at either end of the bridge. When she was picked up, drivers said she seemed extremely nervous, saying she had to get to the other end of the bridge. Some drivers tried to calm her, but upon turning around to face her, they say she was gone. Other motorists claimed to have picked up a woman in white who demanded to know if they accepted Jesus Christ as their savior, then disappeared.

What was particularly strange about these accounts was that many of the drivers were not Floridians and were totally unfamiliar with any ghostly tales. One out-of-state truck driver declared that he gave a lift to a woman, dressed all in white, who was soaking wet and who seemed desperate to get to the opposite end of the long bridge. But while he concentrated on his driving, she had simply vanished by the time he looked again.

One young woman broke the pattern in 2002. She had been to church, but religion didn't change her mind about what she decided she must do. When she started her swan dive from the top of the bridge, she was dressed all in black, from her shiny dress down to her pumps. However, as she fell, she changed her mind—too late, of course—but unlike most of the other jumpers, she didn't die. Still, crashing into the water was excruciating, and her clothes were torn from her body. Fortunate to be rescued quickly, she was rushed to a hospital where she spent months recovering from a broken back, two dislocated shoulders, ruptured bowels, and numerous cuts and bruises, which left her much time to think. In the end, she decided life was worth living after all.

Thankfully, there have been no other major Sunshine Skyway Bridge disasters of the caliber of the 1980 calamities, but the mournful course of suicide attempts continues, as do the reports

STATE ARCHIVES OF FLORIDA K893521

Aerial view showing old and new Sunshine Skyway bridges

of ghostly sightings. It has been suggested that Pinellas County claim ownership of the title "Ghost Coast."

Numerous plans have been proposed to try to prevent as many suicidal jumps from the bridge as possible. In 1999, authorities installed six boxes containing emergency telephones at the top of the bridge. Some potential jumpers have been talked down, but not all people intent on dying want to use them. Consideration was given to installing a fence, but the cost was prohibitive, plus it might possibly make the bridge less safe in high winds. Nets were voted down as possible detriments to sea birds.

In an attempt to address the problem in 2000, off-duty highway patrol troopers started full-time patrols, sometimes parking their cars at the top of the bridge with lights flashing in hopes of discouraging would-be jumpers. Talking to the would-be jumpers is succeeding at least in part.

Lest anyone assume the number of jumpers has decreased as time passes, from January to early August 2012, nineteen people are reported to have jumped from the bridge. One survived.

Some occurrences might be excluded in discussions of the curse of the Sunshine Skyway Bridge, but from the beginning, along with persistent numbers of people intent on killing themselves, the bridge did seem to attract bizarre, if not spooky phenomena.

There was the sad accident in 2005 when a man, who was said to be a heavy drinker but a decent person who lived alone in a modest motel, was crossing a four-lane highway about three miles from the Sunshine Skyway Bridge, apparently on his way to a McDonald's. He was struck by a Chevy Malibu with enough force that one of his legs was severed and fell to the pavement while the rest of his body slammed up onto the roof of the car, his head and shoulders smashed through the splintered windshield. The driver of the car, a ninety-three-year-old man, drove on until he reached a tollbooth at the bridge, unaware of what had happened.

The tollbooth worker thought it was an elaborate prank, perhaps an early Halloween shenanigan, until she saw blood. The driver, not knowing he had been in an accident, seemed to surmise that the body—partly in, partly out of his car—had fallen from the sky. He was taken to a medical facility to await his son, who was already on his way from his home in the far west. The son was aware that his father's dementia was worsening and that he should no longer live alone, but tragically, the son arrived too late.

It is not only boats and cars that run into mysterious difficulties in the area. On a Sunday afternoon in 1996, motorists on the Sunshine Skyway Bridge were terrified when a small plane, engines sputtering, hurtled into the bay at the southern end of the causeway. Several reliable witnesses reported the accident to Coast Guard authorities, who immediately launched rescue helicopters. But even though visibility was good that day, nothing—no plane, no bodies, no debris—was found then or at any other time.

In 1997, in one of the more bizarre Sunshine Skyway incidents, a Fort Lauderdale bartender and four friends tried to perform a pendulum swing bungee jump off the bridge that ended in disaster. The group drove in a stretch limousine to the top of the bridge, where they had previously made arrangements to assure their exploit would be photographed for posterity. Unseen, they quickly rigged a cable, attached it to their harnesses, and leaped over the side of the bridge, hopefully to fame and fortune. Unfortunately, the leader had failed to accurately compute several parts of his plan, the cable snapped, and five daredevils hurtled about seventy feet into Tampa Bay, resulting in broken vertebrae, bruised ribs, and other injuries, but the entire group was fortunate to be alive. Although they did gain some measure of fame when the film of their stunt was televised, as yet, no one has tried to duplicate the group's attempted stunt, nor have the friends thus far demonstrated any move to try it again.

No lives were lost and no ghosts appeared in 1998, when a father and his nine-year-old son survived an accident on the bridge that left them shaken and thankful for their lives. The father had borrowed a front-end loader from a friend to do some work on his property. He had loaded it onto a trailer, which he pulled behind his own medium-sized truck for the trip home. Just as they reached the top of the Sunshine Skyway Bridge, a semi-trailer barreled past them in the next lane, causing a violent wind. The father's trailer fishtailed, hit the side of the bridge, bounced several times with enough force to break the heavy chains that had secured the tractor and trailer, both of which went over the side of the bridge and plunged 170 feet below. Badly shaken, the man and his son still had much to be grateful for—that the chains had broken was fortunate. Troopers from the highway patrol investigated, saying no one had ever seen any circumstance when wind blew such heavy equipment off the bridge.

A recent incident that could have ended tragically might prove that not all the accidents connected to the bridge are ordained to end that way. A forty-seven-year-old man who was fishing from the south fishing pier slipped and fell into the bay. He was rescued by the Coast Guard, checked by paramedics onshore, pronounced uninjured, and sent home.

Investigators determined that he had slipped on the sardines he was using for bait and fell into the water. Possibly a part of the curse, too?

Despite all the tragedies associated with the bridge, there remains the beauty and splendor of the golden superstructure that rises like two sails directing the bridge out to sea. Few man-made works can capture people's attention like the breathtaking view of miles of open water from the top of the Sunshine Skyway Bridge.

CHAPTER 13

Murder on Ocean Drive

Miami's South Beach—sometimes described as an intemperate, irreligious, insomnious, anything-goes Babylon—was unaccustomedly shocked on July 15, 1997, when her adored adopted son, Gianni Versace, was savagely gunned down on the front steps of his Mediterranean-style mansion in broad daylight. Who would dare to commit such a brazen crime? How did the world-famous designer's killer manage to escape through the crowds of bikini-clad sun worshippers on Ocean Drive?

News of the sensational mystery roared through the world of fashion, sports, and entertainment that coalesced on the island of instant gratification known as Miami Beach. Even when the mystery of "Who?" and "Where is he hiding?" was solved, the "Why?" has never been answered.

The status of Miami Beach has soared and sunk more than once since the legendary Carl Fisher built the island in the early 1900s. Its fortunes boomed in the 1920s, crashed with the devastating 1926 hurricane, and climbed again in the '40s and '50s partly due to the popularity of the Arthur Godfrey and Jackie Gleason radio and television shows. Frank Sinatra added glitz and glamour in the '50s and '60s when he and his Rat Pack played the Fontainebleau.

Then in the 1970s, the Beach once more endured bad times. It was considered a crime-infested area where dwindling numbers of die-hard snowbirds returned yearly to escape northern winters and frail, mainly Jewish elders lived out their retirements in or near poverty. Even so, the roller-coaster started another climb in the early 1980s when fashion photographers discovered Florida's dazzling winter sunlight. In 1984, the T-shirt and pastel sports coat attire worn by the leading men in television's *Miami Vice* exploded across the country. The Beach attracted fashion experts and celebrities from South America, Asia, and Europe, including Italy's Gianni Versace. South Beach earned and celebrated its reputation as the American Casablanca.

Gianni Versace, his brother, Santo, and his sister, Donatella, had all followed their mother into the fashion industry and in time, made the family name a leader in the business. As Gianni's reputation grew, he became couturier to high society, Hollywood royalty, and rock stars. Numbered among the designers who consulted periodically for *Miami Vice,* Gianni was drawn to Miami's golden sunlight, the restoration movement in the Beach's Art Deco District, the flood of new restaurants, and the influx of the hip, the rich, and the glamorous.

He decided he must have a South Beach home—he owned three or four other homes but wanted to spend more time where people knew how to have fun. In the early 1990s, he bought a three-story home on Ocean Drive, as well as the small hotel next door, for $2.9 million. He had renovations done on both structures that reportedly cost $30 million and included an added south wing, an elaborate garden, and a stunning pool constructed with more than a million Italian mosaic tiles and twenty-four-karat gold pieces.

The ensuing whirlwind of flashy houseguests coming to the dazzling dinner parties at his Casa Casuarina (named for a casuarina tree on the property) included Sylvester Stallone, Madonna, Princess Diana, and Elton John.

As the number of fashion shoots reached into the thousands, the reputation of South Beach soared, contributing millions of dollars to the local economy. Movie star Michael Caine opened a restaurant, as did Gloria Estefan and her husband, Emilio. The glitter and glow captivated the chic and the chic aspirers.

All of which was exactly what was craved by a young man with a genius-level IQ, a former altar boy with a photographic memory who spoke several languages and possessed an exceptional knowledge of the fine arts. He traveled by car from his home in San Diego and drove across the country, making stops in Minnesota, Chicago, and New Jersey before he finally ceased his journey in Miami. During the stops he made as he crossed the continent, he shot four men dead.

His name was Andrew Cunanan, and he was twenty-seven years old, gay, and a pathological liar. Mental illness was prevalent in his family, and he was a heavy user of drugs, a dangerous combination. Over the years, he told various friends he had met Versace in San Francisco, which possibly was true, but that part remains a mystery even now.

On Tuesday, July 15, Gianni Versace followed his usual morning routine. He walked along busy Ocean Drive, four blocks from his home to the News Cafe. It was a popular bar, cafe, and newsstand where he bought coffee, some magazines, and the Italian newspapers he enjoyed. The sun was shining, the walk pleasant. He must have felt a measure of satisfaction when he returned to his luxurious mansion around 8:40 a.m., climbed the steps, and fitted his key into the lock on the wrought-iron gate.

Waiting on the other side of the street and observing the designer's movements was Cunanan, dressed in shorts and a T-shirt and wearing a baseball cap. He crossed Ocean Drive, climbed part way up the steps of the designer's mansion, pointed

Gianni Versace mansion, South Beach, Miami, Florida

WIKIMEDIA COMMONS

his gun at the back of Versace's neck, fired once into his victim's brain, then again into the side of his skull when Versace turned slightly as he fell.

Task completed, the killer turned and calmly walked away down the street.

Almost immediately, Antonio D'Amico, Gianni's longtime partner, flung open the door and flew to where the fallen Versace's blood was rapidly spreading over the steps. Frozen in horror, bystanders watched the murderer disappear down Ocean Drive.

The killer entered an alley, which led to a nearby five-story parking garage. There, he changed his clothes, dropped them beside a red pickup truck, and took off again on foot.

The Miami Beach police reached the murder scene within seventeen minutes, but medics at Jackson Memorial Hospital pronounced Versace dead at 9:21 a.m.

The victim—gay, wealthy, famous, and beloved—was everything the killer had wanted to be all of his life. So, why did he fire those lethal shots? Was it jealousy? Or was it more complicated than that? Was AIDS involved? The Mafia? Rumors flew.

Andrew Cunanan's long journey had begun in San Diego, his hometown. His mother, MaryAnn, was described as moody, mentally fragile, and as possessing a dark side even in childhood. Pete, the father, originally from the Philippines, was a career navy man turned stockbroker. Having a volatile temper, in time he turned abusive. One year after the 1987 stock market crash, he abandoned his wife and four children to return to the Philippines.

The situation in the Cunanan home was consistently tense and touchy. Still, San Diego was home, and years later, it was where Andrew met someone who became very special to him—a young Minneapolis architect in town on business for a few days, David Madson.

Madson was known among family and friends as a Boy-Scout type who liked helping others and hated violence. He traveled on business frequently and told friends he and Andrew hit it off right away.

Another of Andrew's best friends was Jeffrey Trail, also a handsome, All-American type, and a former navy officer. When Trail moved to Minnesota after Madson's return there, Cunanan's jealous suspicions about the two friends were aroused, and he made a hurried trip to Minneapolis. His gut feelings proved correct. Jeff and David had clicked instantly, both becoming somewhat uncomfortable in Andrew's increasingly erratic presence.

On April 29, 1997, a mutilated body was discovered in David Madson's apartment, the skull smashed with a claw hammer an estimated twenty-seven times, the assailant unknown. When David was absent from work for four days without calling, coworkers persuaded the caretaker of his apartment to use her key to open their friend's unit. Immediately, the overwhelming odor of a decomposing body assaulted them. The swollen body rolled up in a rug on the floor was at first assumed to be Madson's, but it was not. It was Jeff Trail, who had only recently "come out" and retired from the military.

The as yet unsuspecting Madson was with Cunanan, on the road in David's red Jeep when authorities correctly identified the body.

Then on May 3, 1997, two fishermen were walking near East Rush Lake, about an hour from Minneapolis. In the tall grass at the edge of the lake, they stumbled on the body of David Madson, shot three times, with one eye blown away. The police spoke with the families and compared notes. Andrew Cunanan was beginning to come under suspicion.

In the meantime, Cunanan drove Madson's Jeep all night to reach Chicago. In the Windy City, a man named Lee Miglin was next in the line of unfortunates.

Miglin was a highly respected upscale real estate developer who started out selling pancake mix from the trunk of his car. His wife, Marilyn, was a former dancer who was well known for marketing her own line of perfumes and makeup to fans on the Home Shopping Network.

From appearances and by reputation, seventy-five-year old Lee and Marilyn were a happily married couple, the parents of a grown daughter, Marlena, and a son, Duke. They were quietly wealthy, well-connected politically and socially.

On May 4, Lee's body was discovered in his garage, brutally stabbed dozens of times in the neck and chest, with deep wounds penetrating his heart. Nearby, the police found a discarded garden saw that had been used to nearly detach the victim's head.

Investigators made little progress until later when someone noted a red Jeep parked near the Miglin residence that had not been moved for three days. A check of the license plate revealed that it belonged to another murder victim. By that time, thanks to the easily traced red Jeep, the perpetrator of the crime was now believed to be Andrew Cunanan.

As soon as authorities connected Cunanan to Miglin's murder, rumors started to swirl, some insinuating that either Lee or his son, Duke, was gay. Others regarded it as a random killing. No previous connections between Miglin and his killer were found to exist. The Miglin family was adamant in denying any ties.

In the meantime, heading toward the East Coast and South on Interstate 95 in Miglin's Lexus, Cunanan must have known he needed to be less conspicuous. He also came to realize that Miglin's car could be tracked electronically, thanks to the way cell phone calls were transmitted from the vehicle. He needed another means of transportation.

Accordingly, after crossing the Delaware Memorial Bridge, he pulled off I-95 at the first exit in New Jersey, stopping at Fort Mott State Park next to a Civil War burial ground. It was a quiet, lonely spot where the caretaker, Bill Reese, became Cunanan's fourth victim in twelve days.

Reese was a quiet, unassuming, forty-two-year-old family man who was proud to have the job of caring for historical burial grounds. He enjoyed the beauty and the peaceful routine of working there every day and returning to his wife and son at home at the same time every evening.

When he didn't come home on May 9, his concerned wife investigated. She found a green Lexus on the grounds but couldn't find Reese anywhere. Alarmed, she phoned her father, who, having heard reports of a dangerous killer in a green Lexus, told her to get out quickly. She did, and then called the police from a safe place.

Within minutes, officers arrived and immediately began to search the grounds. Shortly, they found her dead husband.

A quick check of the license plate on the Lexus revealed who it was they were looking for, and it was obvious the killer had escaped in the victim's red pickup truck.

Even with twelve law enforcement groups, including the FBI, on the lookout for him, Cunanan succeeded in speeding down I-95 in the bright red pickup all the way to Miami, a melting pot of transients from South America, Russia, the Caribbean, New York, Italy, and just about everywhere else. Miami was also famous for being a place where all those people from all those places melded together and minded their own business. It was the perfect spot for a young, dark-complexioned man to hide.

As soon as he arrived, Andrew took a room at a low-rent hotel, where he existed for two months on takeout food and occupied much of his time buying and reading books and magazines. *Vanity Fair,* the high fashion magazine said to have been one of his favorites, frequently reported on the doings of Gianni

Versace, a lifestyle for which Cunanan fervently yearned. Perhaps he was making plans even then.

On June 12, Cunanan's face became well known to law enforcement agencies all over the country. He made the FBI's Ten Most Wanted List, with photos of him circulated everywhere. To his advantage, they were photos taken before he had gained some weight, making him less recognizable.

On July 15, with his backpack on his shoulder and without paying his last day's rent, he left the hotel and walked to Ocean Drive, across the street from the Casa Casuarina, and waited.

Inconspicuously hidden in his hand was Jeff Trail's gun, a .40-caliber handgun, the same one that would eventually be proved to have ended the lives of Trail, Madson, and Reese. At 8:40 a.m., the gun ended the life of Gianni Versace.

By 8:55 a.m., the Miami Beach police swarmed onto the scene, and within seconds, it seemed, the media appeared.

Following up on interviews with bystanders, the police searched the nearby parking garage, where they found the red pickup truck with the pile of clothes and backpack Cunanan had shed. The truck, they learned, belonged to William Reese, the New Jersey cemetery caretaker. A few more hours of solid detective work put the pieces together to solve the question of "Who killed Versace?" The mystery remained as to where the murderer was hiding.

Hundreds of people crowded the South Beach street outside Versace's home, staring at the blood-stained steps as news of his murder swept the country. The Florida Department of Law Enforcement joined with FBI agents on one of the largest manhunts in their history.

At a joint news conference, police and FBI agents cautioned the public that the killer was a menace to everyone, not only gays. In describing Cunanan as well educated, well dressed, and extremely articulate, they admitted that, since they were unsure of his motivation, everyone should be on guard.

Worthless leads flooded in from Brazil, Canada, and even as far away as Switzerland. Half the world's population, it seemed, had spotted Andrew Cunanan somewhere. The actions of the increasingly aggressive media forced the Miami Beach police to stop use of their radios as reporters and broadcasters were monitoring them closely. Any suggestion of new information dispersed over the airwaves caused an onslaught of cameras and microphones to descend onto the scene whether or not it was warranted.

Except for a few close friends, almost everyone who ever had any contact with Cunanan obliged the tabloids with all the details they could recall and some they fabricated. Everyone, of course, expected generous compensation.

Andrew's mother was heavily medicated and moved into a witness protection program. His father, still in the Philippines and in denial about his Catholic, altar boy son, refused to believe any of the sordid details he heard. Neither parent had any idea as to the whereabouts of their notorious offspring.

Among the thousands of boats in the Miami Beach area, some huge, some bizarre, some nondescript, it takes a truly outstanding or unique vessel to attract much attention. The small, pale blue houseboat berthed at Indian Creek was gaudy, but not eye-catching enough to draw much notice among the huge number of watercraft in the neighborhood where it was docked. It belonged to a German nightclub owner, who lived most of the time in Las Vegas and depended on Fernando Carreira, a seventy-one-year-old caretaker, to look after the boat, checking on it every two weeks or so during the owner's absence.

Carreira looked after other properties, too. Late in the afternoon of July 23, while he was making his rounds with his wife, he stopped for a look at the pale blue houseboat when he noticed the upper lock appeared to have been tampered with. When he attempted to open the lower lock, he discovered it was unlocked. That was when the caretaker realized that the drapes, which were ordinarily kept open, were closed.

Suspecting a trespasser must be on board, Carreira cautiously continued farther inside. He reached for the handgun he always carried on his rounds, and as he did, a shot rang out from the upper level of the houseboat.

Later, it would be surmised that Cunanan had heard Carreira's footsteps, assumed the law had finally caught him, and ended his own life with the same gun that he had used on Trail, Madson, Reese, and Versace.

At the first sound of the gunshot, the caretaker grabbed his wife's hand and pulled her outside where they hid and phoned their son, who in turn alerted authorities. Within minutes, the police blocked traffic on Collins Avenue, helicopters hovered overhead, and curious residents of the nearby luxury hotels hung out over their balconies, stretching to see the action.

The Metro-Dade Special Response Team boarded the blue houseboat at 8:20 p.m. and found a dead man on the second floor, with Jeff Trail's gun, the gun that killed Gianni Versace, in his hand and a gunshot wound in his head. The drawn-out mystery of where Andrew Cunanan was hiding was over.

Gianni Versace's funeral attracted as many celebrities as his parties had when he was alive. Among the notables were Luciano Pavarotti, Princess Diana, Sting, Elton John, and Carolyn Bessette-Kennedy. His brother and sister escorted Versace's ashes back to Italy.

The houseboat caretaker, Fernando Carreira, collected a forty-five-thousand-dollar reward.

The poorly kept blue houseboat became a one-time movie set and a lure for sightseers before it broke loose and sank at its mooring a few months later.

Casa Casuarina has since been turned into an exclusive, ten-room hotel where the least expensive room goes for $1,400 a night in the off-season. Even now, a day seldom goes by that a few tourists do not stop to snap a photo of themselves in front of the former Versace mansion.

CHAPTER 14

Ancient Mystery Surrounded by Skyscrapers

When Bob Carr drove over the Brickell Bridge in downtown Miami one morning in May 1998, he observed some disturbing activity below. A demolition team was dismantling six apartment buildings on the south side of the Miami River where it flows into Biscayne Bay. Carr, a Miami archaeologist, knew a routine archaeological survey had to be done before construction could begin in any area with possible archaeological or preservation significance, and he knew this site should certainly be evaluated.

Carr, who had lived in Miami since he was a young boy, became interested in the city's archaeology in grade school. After graduating from Florida State University, he was named Miami-Dade County's first archaeologist. Understandably, he was greatly troubled to see the activity at Brickell Point.

After Carr made a few phone calls and wrote some letters to the proper authorities, the developer, Michael Baumann, agreed to postpone the planned construction of two forty-story towers on the 2.2-acre site long enough for a routine archaeological survey to be done. Carr and a team from the Miami-Dade Historic Preservation Division wasted no time in starting the project.

Under the direction of field director John Ricisak, a crew of professionals and volunteers began work on an area where footer trenches had already been dug. With the strict time limit always at the back of their minds, the workers cleared away several feet of debris and were surprised to find numerous holes cut into the oolitic limestone slab under the soil. Were they natural or man-made? The team could not agree.

One surveyor, Ted Riggs, observing an arclike section, believed the holes could be part of a large circular pattern. He calculated the circle might be about thirty-eight feet in diameter. Using red paint, he made an outline on the ground where he thought the circle would be.

With the agreed-upon deadline looming, the team brought a bulldozer to the site to move the topsoil. Then working by hand, they dug almost two feet deep along the red line Riggs had drawn. They were amazed to find a perfect circle of holes or basins, just as he had projected. In all, there were twenty-four large oblong holes, two to three feet long and about one-and-a-half feet deep, six smaller ones, and hundreds of smaller round holes scattered about. Three of the large holes seemed to have been placed in lines as if to mark north, south and east, with the eastern one looking much like a human eye.

Working against the clock, the team did its best to keep the discovery a secret to prevent curiosity seekers from swarming the site and possibly damaging or carrying off material that might be valuable in solving the mystery. As the excavation proceeded, they found many more artifacts—a five-foot-long shark skeleton, its head facing west, shells, ceramics, bones, the carapace of a sea turtle, a dolphin skull, a silver thimble, and several teeth from an extinct type of seal.

The location of all this excitement, Brickell Point, was named for William Brickell, one of Miami's founders who in the 1800s operated Brickell's Trading Post there. That Seminole Indians frequently traded at the post was proven by the beads and coins the team sifted from the earth at the circle. Among the hundreds of articles found were two stone axes constructed of basalt, a volcanic rock found in the Appalachian Mountains. The team also uncovered two specimens made of galena, a highly prized mineral of lead sulfite, which Native Americans fashioned into beads and ornaments. It was a rare substance found mostly in Missouri, Illinois, and Kentucky that was frequently used in trading. All the artifacts the team uncovered in the circle indicated how extensively trade had been carried on so long ago.

Then in December 1998, a *Miami Herald* photographer happened to walk across Brickell Bridge, and the secret was out—in a big way. The *Herald* carried the story, which national news services immediately picked up, inspiring crowds of souvenir hunters to descend on the site. Although the developer quickly had a fence installed and hired security personnel to stand guard, souvenir hunters weren't the only ones paying attention. The news media were joined by all sorts of protest groups determined to preserve the Miami Circle, as it became known. A conglomeration of demonstrators—New Agers, preservationists, environmentalists, white Americans, black Americans, Cubans, Cub Scouts, Native Americans, skilled professionals, and Joe Six-Packers, singing, making speeches, carrying candles, beating drums—all demanded that America's Stonehenge, as some called it, be preserved.

Teachers brought schoolchildren. Several Buddhist monks clambered over the fence but were ousted by police. Helicopters hovered overhead. Television producers were beside themselves, vying with each other for the latest news to present on *Good Morning America,* the *Today* show, CNN, and even the BBC.

Miami, the ever-changing, touristy, Art Deco, Little Havana, yacht-filled city, just might have the most important Native American treasure in North America, and sign-carrying demonstrators were not about to let it to be destroyed.

However, it was still Miami. People offered opinions, revelations known only to them, and unconventional theories guaranteed to solve the mystery of the Miami Circle. Possibly the least attractive explanation was that the circle was simply the remains of an old septic tank that had been connected to the demolished apartment buildings. That was proven wrong, but it was sometimes impossible to disprove other theories. That it was a corner marker for the legendary Bermuda Triangle, for example. Or that it was somehow connected to Atlantis, the mythical island sunk beneath the Atlantic Ocean. One woman phoned Bob Carr to inform him that the circle was an ancient UFO landing pad. A man in Australia warned that damaging the circle would result in a disruption of the Earth's energy so that the Earth would wobble and become unbalanced and top-heavy, making the equator run north and south and causing widespread disasters.

Truly, the discovery of the long-buried Miami Circle captivated people from around the world. With populations and economies growing, more and more valuable relics of past societies are being lost to development everywhere, not just in the United States. Many voiced concern that this finding be preserved for its irreplaceable historic value.

Michael Baumann, the developer who had paid $8.5 million for the Brickell Point property, was growing impatient. He generously offered to pay to have experts move the circle to another location, a park perhaps.

Baumann, a Miami native and the son of a developer, was no stranger to controversy. Enemies he made during a previous similar rumpus remain bitter to this day about that episode, even though Baumann lost the decision in the dispute. Bob Carr, however, said Baumann was as cooperative as any developer with whom he had dealt. Carr believes cooperation leads to less risk to future sites.

Mayor Joe Carollo thought moving the circle was a good idea, since it would save the more than $1 million of property taxes the planned condo towers could bring to the city and the county. Of that money, it was estimated that the Miami-Dade County government would take in $647,000, with more than $900,000 going to the Miami-Dade County school district. The mayor said, "I have the responsibility to do what is right for past civilizations. But I have a greater responsibility to the present civilization." Additionally, while considerable sums of badly needed revenue could be lost by stopping the development at Brickell Point, there were legitimate concerns that developers could move even more valuable projects out of Miami—where archaeological regulations are strict—to other sites less likely to hold artifacts and therefore not subject to rigid regulations. Miami could suffer an even greater loss of revenue. It was a sticky situation.

A medicine man who had led a group of Seminoles from Oklahoma spoke for many when he declared that removing the circle from the rock where it had been carved would be the same as destroying it. Though most archaeologists involved agreed that the circle would lose much of its scientific worth if it were moved, they were afraid that moving it might be the best they could expect—unless officials acted quickly to take ownership through eminent domain.

In February 1999, the Miami-Dade County Commission voted to use eminent domain to acquire the land around the Miami Circle. Eminent domain requires a landowner to sell a property to the government, providing it can be demonstrated that the property is necessary for a specific purpose.

Baumann, who was eager to get construction started, gave the go-ahead to Bob Carr to hire an expert help to move the circle. Carr hired Joshua Billig, a respected stonemason from Rockers Stone and Supply who was known for his work with natural South Florida stone. Moving the huge Miami Circle would be a new kind of challenge, and Billig accepted it eagerly.

Joshua Billig was the younger brother of Amy Billig, a teenager who vanished from a busy Coconut Grove street in 1974, and whose story is told in a previous chapter, "Search for Amy." Joshua Billig had only recently come to accept the belief of his friends and relatives that his chosen vocation—building stone walls, some of the most beautiful in Miami—was directly related to the impact his sister's disappearance had on his early ideal family life, a heinous crime that occupied his parents, heart and soul, for the rest of their lives. Undoubtedly, moving the Miami Circle would be a challenging variation in the work he enjoyed so much.

At least it seemed that way in the beginning. But as the demonstrating crowds grew almost daily, and telephone calls from friends and strangers begging Billig not to take the job never seemed to stop, he began having second thoughts.

A conversation with Bobby C. Billie, spiritual leader of the Independent Traditional Seminoles, finally changed Billig's mind. Billie, who had been keeping a vigil at the circle, told Joshua that he should not to be involved in moving it. For every sacred Indian site that is destroyed, Billie said, some sort of destruction will take place somewhere in the world. Although Billig was not totally convinced about what Billie said, he was still disturbed.

After listening to the various Native Americans gathered at the site, Billig came to believe he might be damaging something important if he went ahead with the job. He made up his mind that night—he did not want to be part of it.

He called Baumann the next morning to resign from the project. One day later, he could hardly help but be pleased when demonstrators at the site joyfully displayed signs proclaiming, "Joshua Billig Is Our Hero."

The delay caused by his resignation provided an opportunity for Miami-Dade officials to begin procedures resulting in a judge issuing a temporary injunction against building on the site. The ball was rolling, and soon the owner offered to sell the 2.2 acres for fifty million dollars. Baumann's offer was not accepted, but after a time, he agreed to lower the price to $26.7 million.

The state kicked in fifteen million dollars, still leaving funds woefully short, but as the deadline for settlement neared, a conservation group based in San Francisco, the Trust for Public Land, offered a loan that made the transaction possible.

In November 1999, the State of Florida Preservation 2000 land acquisition program took the unconventional and extraordinary step of buying the property from Baumann for his price, the money having been obtained through state funds and various donations.

The Historical Museum of Southern Florida then finalized a forty-four-year lease with Florida's Department of State to provide public access to the Miami Circle and to ensure its continued preservation.

While the negotiations and demonstrations were going on, the serious work of archaeological investigation continued. So many questions demanded answers. How old was the circle? Who built it? What was its purpose?

John Ricisak, from the County Historic Preservation Division, sent two charcoal fragments, one from inside one basin and another from the midden in the circle, to be carbon-dated. The results, along with other tests, convinced most local archaeologists that the circle is at least 1,800 to 2,000 years old, although some believe it might be as many as 10,000 to 13,000 years old.

With these dates in mind, it mostly became accepted that the people who built the Miami Circle were an indigenous Native American tribe called the Tequesta. They were a small group of approximately one thousand who lived around the mouth of the Miami River.

Brickell Point is believed to have been part of the area where the Tequesta built their village on both sides of the Miami River, a region abundant in aquatic life. The Tequesta were not farmers; rather, they fished, hunted, and gathered the area's plentiful fruits and local plants for their food. Ravaged by wars and diseases from exposure to European explorers, the last of the tribe is thought to have left the area about 1763, but there is no proof of that.

Most archaeologists believe the Miami Circle was the location of a temple or council house, or possibly the home of a Tequesta chief. That the animal bones and excellent tools uncovered there might have been offerings for a ceremonial house of some kind is another theory. The oblong basins were probably used for wooden support posts. But whatever it was to the Tequestas, Bob Carr stated that nothing like it has ever been found before.

Ricisak added, "For many people in South Florida there is a sense of rootlessness, a lack of a sense of history. We now know there is history here."

In addition, even though it is located in a "tear-it-down-and-build-something-new city," the Brickell Point property contains

COURTESY OF FLORIDARAMBLER.COM

Photo of Miami Circle Park in March 2011

prehistoric midden deposits on 50 to 75 percent of the area. Amazingly, archaeologists estimate that 85 percent of the circle is intact—this in a site of frequent construction and demolition.

The circle's local, regional, statewide, and national significance is assured by the fact that it is the only known prehistoric work cut into bedrock in the United States, and it is the oldest known permanent settlement on the East Coast of the United States.

On February 2, 2002, the Miami Circle was listed on the National Register of Historic Places, and on January 16, 2009, it was further honored by being named a National Historic Landmark.

Work began on how to prepare and preserve the site for public viewing. The state hired an Orlando architectural firm to draft a plan for a park to surround the circle. Its location, at the mouth of a river in the downtown of a busy, always developing city would be most welcome to workers and residents, since there is so little inviting, accessible green space in downtown Miami.

One complication arose when a portion of the seawall that bordered the site collapsed into the Miami River, but that was repaired. However, workers were dismayed when they noticed some deterioration to the circle, due to exposure after the many delays.

In 2003, to protect the circle, workers installed a coating of limestone over it, which was planned to be only temporary, while officials determined the best way to preserve the priceless artifact. A type of Native American–looking hut with a thatched roof was considered, as was some sort of clear plastic roof. More funding would be needed, whenever and whatever improvements would be decided upon. Not everyone was pleased when word spread that the circle would be covered up, with some arguing that making a trip to see the historic site would be a disappointment since it was covered up.

Florida's state archaeologist, Ryan Wheeler, made the decision that covering the circle was the best solution. When he watched the holes in the circle fill with water from the rising water table, he realized that at the present time, it was the only way to preserve it. The hope is that perhaps in the future, archaeologists will have other technologies that will be more satisfying to the public.

In February 2011, a grand opening ceremony formally raised the curtain on the Miami Circle Park, featuring a Native American ritual.

For now, Miami's newest park has been built around its famous circle, which lies buried beneath several layers of dirt. It is a precious open space with a slightly depressed constructed ring to represent what lies below. The ring has stones set into it to mark the twenty-four limestone basins in the circle, and chunks of white limestone scattered irregularly around the circle serve as benches for anyone wanting to enjoy the gorgeous view of the Miami River. Low, tastefully done signs explain some of the site's history to visitors who are unaware of it.

A new river walk connects at the base of Brickell Bridge, which is adjacent to the park. It follows along the south side of the Miami River, on to Biscayne Bay.

One evening a week, every week since it was discovered, a Native American spiritualist, Catherine Hummingbird Ramirez, has held a candlelight vigil at the site, during which she spreads a blessing over the circle, giving thanks to the Great Spirit.

For most people, the park is a place to remember the importance of the Miami Circle not only to Florida's Native Americans, but also to modern Miami citizens who are from all over the world but who forgot their differences and came together to save the circle. It is a welcome and peaceful breath of fresh air in a busy city —and it only took about two thousand years to find.

CHAPTER 15

Good Food, Pranks, and Ghosts at the Desert Inn

Among the constant stream of people who have moved to Florida over the years, there are those who did not primarily come for the sun and surf, the South Beach night-life, or the theme-park attractions. Some came to work on the cattle ranches, citrus groves, turpentine camps, or fishing trawlers. Others moved here because of family connections. Beverly Zicheck, from Texas, belongs to the latter group.

Beverly visited her parents, Stephanie and George Zicheck, when they bought the Desert Inn in Yeehaw Junction in 1986 and decided she liked the area so much that she took over running the place in 1987 when her parents moved on. As the new owner, Beverly made a point of personally greeting all of her customers, many of them old-timers in the region. By encouraging them to sign a register and join her in long conversations, she learned much about the history of the Desert Inn and the neighboring area. The more she learned, the more fascinated she became.

She was told that parts of the inn were probably built in the late 1880s, in the heart of Florida cattle country, surrounded by wilderness, which is mostly how it remains today. Henry Flagler extended his East Coast Railroad through the area in the 1900s, making it easier to move timber from a nearby sawmill, as well as ship other freight. In the Yeehaw Junction area, Flagler built a small depot and a trading post, which eventually became the Desert Inn. Lumbermen, traders, cowmen, and other locals gathered at the inn to let off steam, drink, eat, and dance. As late as the 1930s, the second floor became known far and wide as a busy bordello, but a dance hall in back was never replaced after it burned to the ground during a fight between two cowmen. Gunfights were not unusual.

It was in the 1930s that a railroad vagabond, Dan Wilson, was forced off a train in Yeehaw Junction. He looked around, apparently liked what he saw, and decided to stay. Somehow, he scraped up the money to buy the shack that was by then called a hotel, "borrowed" some railroad timber he needed to add some rooms, and the Desert Inn was born.

The inn at Yeehaw Junction, the only "place of refreshment" for the vast wild area, was frequented by cowmen, Seminole Indians, moonshiners, lumbermen, and occasional businessmen. When the roads were finally paved, tourists began making stops there, too, apparently relieved to come upon some vestige of what passed for civilization in the middle of nowhere.

Some believe Yeehaw Junction's name came from the Seminole Indians, whose word for wolf is *yeehaw*. Although wolves were plentiful in the area in early days, others insist that *yeehaw* refers to the sound made by donkeys, many of which were used for work in the region at that time. Despite the opinion battle, it's an undisputed fact that the tiny spot on the map in Osceola County with a population of 240 was originally called Jackass Crossing. When the Florida Turnpike was constructed and needed an exit name to print on maps, and the Greyhound Line also needed a name to publish for its stop there, Jackass Crossing was considered unsuitable. Yeehaw Junction was the name chosen, but Jackass Crossing is still heard among old-timers and long-distance truck drivers on their CB radios.

Located at the intersection of Florida State Road 60 and US 441 and only a few miles from the turnpike, Yeehaw Junction has become a sometimes desperately needed stopping-off place for travelers relieved to discover the Desert Inn with its row of motel-style cabins at the west side of the main building. Economical prices and no-frills accommodations attract long-distance truck drivers from the turnpike, hunters, fishermen, and the occasional tourists who may be pleasantly surprised by the friendly folks and the good "Cracker" food at the inn. (For the unfamiliar, the term "cracker" refers to Floridians whose families have deep roots in the state's history. It's commonly thought that "cracker" derives from the early cowboys' practice of cracking their whips to herd or capture cattle.) The turtle burgers, frog dinners, biscuits, and chili—all homemade—draw rave reviews.

Fred and Julie Cheverette owned the inn before Beverly's parents, and from all reports, the couple gained a reputation for being good-natured and good-humored. Julie particularly enjoyed pulling tricks on people and became somewhat famous for one in particular: She had fishing lines stretched across the restaurant ceiling in all directions with rubber spiders or other creepy crawlers attached at the ends of the lines above seats at the bar, the tables, or the booths. When the time seemed right, one of the fake critters was dropped on an unsuspecting customer for excitement, laughs, and the occasional fright, as when one customer screamed and tore out of the building so forcefully that the door needed to be repaired. Most of the critters are still there and are still used when the time seems right.

Just to keep things interesting, the Cheverettes also installed a very lifelike American Indian mannequin couple and their baby in a corner booth, where they remain. A functioning jukebox helps preserve the atmosphere of the recent past.

Atmosphere, good food, historical interest—what more would a stopping-off place possibly have to interest patrons? Perhaps something they might not expect and might not be so enthusiastic about, but when a structure or parts of it have been around since the 1880s, inevitably a great deal of history is attached to it, and not all of that history is pleasant.

Speeding motorists on the turnpike and interstate highway crossroads just a stone's throw from the inn have produced more than occasional fatalities over the years. In addition, combining tough men relaxing after long days of backbreaking work with guns on their hips and free-flowing booze has resulted in the occasional gunfight victim, too.

Moreover, Beverly Zicheck learned that several suicides have occurred at the inn, including one in the 1900s when a man, apparently distraught over being jilted by his lover, turned his gun on himself while lying in bed in a second-floor room. More recently, one morning Beverly was shocked to find a man who had hung himself from a ceiling pipe the night before. Some regulars at the inn believe the fatalities in and around the vicinity are responsible for the ghostly phenomena familiar to people who have worked there over the years.

The upstairs rooms are closed for now, kept locked from everyone except for Beverly and her employees. Some rooms are strictly for storage, but the rooms formerly used by ladies of the night are pretty much as they were and are being turned into a small museum. However, it seems doors known to be locked can sometimes be heard opening and closing. Sometimes whispers come from unoccupied rooms. At other times, footsteps are heard coming from upstairs when the door at the bottom of the steps is closed and locked. Objects on the second floor have moved overnight when no one had been on that floor. Once, a large desk moved from one side of the room to the opposite side when access to the upstairs was locked. There was even one report of a man's ghost seen walking into the inn and simply disappearing. Some employees have become so spooked that they refuse to go to the second floor for any reason.

Beverly, a history fan, decided early on that she wanted to do what she could to preserve the small bit of Florida history she had in her possession. She began to investigate what was necessary to have the Desert Inn listed in the National Register of Historic Places, knowing it wouldn't be easy. She was right about that. To qualify, she had to first prove the place was more than fifty years old and had no major structural modifications.

She began a search of any records she could find and interviewed every source that seemed reliable, all with little results. After two discouraging years, Beverly consulted her state representative, Irio "Bud" Bronson. He put her in touch with the people in Tallahassee who could help her meet the requirements. In January 1994, Beverly's hard work paid off. The Desert Inn in Yeehaw Junction was listed in the National Register of Historic Places, with an impressive sign installed in front of the building.

It seemed a happy ending for this icon of old Cracker Florida, but unfortunately, that wasn't quite the case. In 2006, a partnership of two developers announced plans to build a self-contained city of one hundred thousand homes on forty-one thousand acres of land directly across the highway from the Desert Inn and they had the funds to do it. Yeehaw Junction would never be the same.

The Florida Department of Community Affairs immediately opposed the plan, as did other state officials who contended that if it were permitted, the development would contribute to

Desert Inn at Yeehaw Junction

GEORGE F. WRIGHT, MD

urban sprawl. Environmentalists breathed a sigh of relief and then relaxed even more when it was revealed that the two developers were involved in lawsuits—against each other—and the proposed "green" city, to have been named Destiny, would be put on hold indefinitely.

Whatever happens across the highway, Beverly Zicheck feels ready to retire and hopes someone will take over running the Desert Inn. She wants to find someone who won't tear the place down and replace it with something shiny and new.

"I just want the building preserved," she says. "I don't want it to get in the wrong hands."

Without a doubt, many Floridians who love the Sunshine State's history, with her ghosts and myths and mysteries, also long to preserve her disappearing Cracker past.

BIBLIOGRAPHY

CHAPTER 1: THE ELUSIVE FLORIDA SKUNK APE

Boone, Christian, and Kathy Jefcoats. "Searching for Bigfoot Group to Sue Georgia Hoaxers." *Atlanta Journal-Constitution,* August 30, 2008.

Interview with Loren Coleman and Cyndi Tyson on *Animal Planet.* November 4, 2010. www.lorencoleman.com/myakka.html.

Otto, Steve. "Absolutely Kinda Irrefutable Proof of Skunk Ape." *Tampa Bay Tribune,* February 13, 2001.

Wilford, John. "Society Formed to Bring Them Back Alive." *New York Times,* January 19, 1982.

CHAPTER 2: FIRST AMERICAN CIVIL RIGHTS MARTYR

Green, Ben. *Before His Time.* Gainesville: University Press of Florida, 1999.

"Slain in Bombing, 1951." *New York Times,* August 20, 2006.

"Suspects Named in Moore's Murder." *Attorney General Consumer Bulletin,* August 24, 2006.

Ward, Kenric. "Harry T. Moore: Ahead of His Time." *Press Journal,* November 9, 2008.

CHAPTER 3: ST. PETERSBURG'S CINDER LADY

Arnold, Larry E. *Ablaze.* New York: M. Evans & Co. Inc., 1995.

Blizin, Jerry. "FBI Said 1951 Death Wasn't 'Spontaneous Combustion,' But Mystery Persists." *St. Petersburg Times,* November 11, 2009.

———. "The Reeser Case." *St. Petersburg Times,* August 9, 1951.

FBI Records: Freedom of Information Act. *Spontaneous Human Combustion.*

Sanders, Jacquin. "Burning Death Remains a Mystery." *St. Petersburg Times,* November 10, 2009.

Snider, John C. "The Joe Nickell Files: Spontaneous Human Combustion." *SciFi Dimensions,* July 2000.

Zucco, Tom. "Hunt for Haunts." *St. Petersburg Times,* October 31, 2002.

CHAPTER 4: THE TRIAL OF RUBY MCCOLLUM

Ellis, C. Arthur Jr., PhD, and Leslie E. Ellis, PhD. *The Trial of Ruby McCollum.* Bloomington, IN: First Books Library, 2003.

Evans, Tammy. *The Silencing of Ruby McCollum: Race, Class, and Gender in the South.* Gainesville: University Press of Florida, 2006.

Hemenway, Robert E. *Zora Neale Hurston.* Champaign: University of Illinois Press, 1980.

Huie, William Bradford. *Woman in the Suwannee Jail.* New York: E. P. Dutton & Co. Inc. 1956.

Newton, Michael. *The Invisible Empire: The Ku Klux Klan in Florida.* Gainesville: University Press of Florida, 2001.

"The Press: Case of Ruby McCollum." *Time,* October 25, 1954.

CHAPTER 5: A TALE OF TWO JUDGES

Bishop, Jim. *The Murder Trial of Judge Peel.* New York: Simon & Schuster, 1962.

"CRIME: The Scoutmaster & The Judge." *Time,* November 14, 1960.

Doe Network: Case File 2267 DMFL. Curtis Eugene Chillingworth (missing since June 14, 1955).

"Judge Chillingworth Murder." Jupiter History Web Home Page. www .jupiter.fl.us/History/Judge-Chillingworth-Murder.cfm.

Musgrave, Jane. "Attorney A. Clark Sentenced to Five Years for Bilking Law Clients." *The Palm Beach Post,* June 7, 2011.

Weiss, Murray, and Bill Hoffman. *Palm Beach Babylon.* New York: Carol Publishing Co., 1992.

CHAPTER 6: ESCAPE FROM A SEA MONSTER

Florida Department of State, Division of Historical Resources. *The USS Massachusetts.*

McCleary, Edward Brian. "My Escape from a Sea Monster." *FATE,* 1965.

New York Times, August 1, 2011.

Niednagel, Jordan. *The Ocean: A World of Mystery.* June 14, 2010. www
.trueauthority.com/cryptozoology/oceanprnt.htm.

CHAPTER 7: DEAD ZONE ON INTERSTATE 4

Carlson, Charlie. *Weird Florida.* New York: Sterling Publishing Co., 2005.

Jenkins, Gregg. *Florida's Ghostly Legends & Haunted Folklore, Vol. 1.*
Sarasota, FL: Pineapple Press, 2005.

Stone, Rick, and Luisa Yanez. "I-95 in Florida Is Nation's Deadliest
Highway." *Palm Beach Post,* June 6, 2010.

Tracy, Dan. "Study: High-Speed Train Would Have Made Money."
Orlando Sentinel, March 9, 2011.

CHAPTER 8: ONE SMALL STEP—OR ONE GIANT HOAX?

Bancroft, Collette. "Lunar Lunacy." *St. Petersburg Times,* September 29, 2002.

Hansen, James R. *First Man: The Life of Neil Armstrong.* New York: Simon
& Schuster, 2005.

National Aeronautics and Space Administration. *Spinoff: NASA Technologies
Enhance Our Lives.*

Reynolds, David West. *Apollo: The Epic Journey to the Moon.* San Diego:
Tehabi Books Inc., 2002.

Schwartz, John. "Vocal Minority Insists It Was All Smoke and Mirrors."
New York Times, July 14, 2009.

Soller, Kurt. "Moonstruck." *Newsweek,* July 17, 2009.

Wagner, Leon. *One Giant Leap.* New York: Tom Doherty Associates, LLC, 2004.

CHAPTER 9: D. B. COOPER'S FLORIDA WIDOW?

Associated Press. "Washington: New Tip Does Not Lead to D.B. Cooper."
New York Times, August 8. 2011.

"The Bandit Who Went Out into the Cold." *Time,* December 6, 1971.

Baskas, Harriet. "Ariel, WA: Whatever Happened to D. B. Cooper?" NPR. December 1, 2008. www.npr.org/templates/story/story .php?storyId=97629326.

Boulé, Margie. "Florida Woman's Search for D.B. Cooper Isn't Business, It's Personal." *Oregonian,* August 3, 2000.

Gladwell, Malcolm. "Safety in the Skies." *The New Yorker,* October 1, 2001, p. 60.

Gunther, Max. *D. B. Cooper: What Really Happened.* Chicago: Contemporary Books Inc., 1985.

Pitts, Byron (reporter). "D.B. Cooper—Found At Last?" *CBS Evening News,* August 22, 2000.

Seelye, Katherine, and Charlie Savage. "Forty Years Later, A Tip with Potential in a Famous Case." *New York Times,* August 2, 2011.

CHAPTER 10: SEARCH FOR AMY

Anapu, Greg, and Susan Billig. *Without a Trace.* New York: Avon Books, 2001.

McClintock, Jack. "Amy's Only Hope." *Sun Sentinel,* December 19, 1993.

Navarro, Mireya. "The Night Caller: 21 Years of Unspeakable Grief." *New York Times,* December 3, 1995.

New York Times, February 4, 1983.

Ovalle, David. "Mother's Death Ends Quest to Find Child." *Grove First,* June 8, 2005.

Smolowe, Jill. "Voice of the Torturer." *Time,* December 18, 1995.

CHAPTER 11: FLORIDA'S OWN CAPTAIN MIDNIGHT

Author's conversation with J. MacDougall, March 1, 2011.

Branscomb, Anne Wells. *Who Owns Information?* New York: Basic Books/ Division of Harper Collins, 1994.

Nice, Karim, and Tom Harris. "How Satellite TV Works." http:// electronics.howstuffworks.com/satellite-tv.htm.

Zoglin, Richard, Jim Byers (Los Angeles), and Jerome Cramer (Washington, D.C.). "Video: Captain Midnight's Sneak Attack." *Time,* May 12, 1986.

Zoglin, Richard, and Jerome Cramer (Washington, D.C., with other bureaus). "Video: Grounding Captain Midnight." *Time,* August 4, 1986.

CHAPTER 12: THE DARK SIDE OF THE SUNSHINE SKYWAY BRIDGE

Brink, Graham. "Pilot in Skyway Disaster Is Dead." *St. Petersburg Times,* September 3, 2002.

Heller, Jean. "The Day the Skyway Fell." *St. Petersburg Times,* May 7, 2000.

———. "Horrific Accident Created an Unforgettable Scene." *St. Petersburg Times,* May 9, 1980.

Herald Tribune, August 15, 2010.

Jenkins, Gregg. *Florida's Ghostly Legends & Haunted Folklore: Vol. I.* Sarasota, FL: Pineapple Press. 2005.

Jones, Jamie. "Skyway Safeguards Don't Deter Jumpers." *St. Petersburg Times,* October 6, 2003.

Mair, George. *Bridge Down.* New York: Stein & Day Publishers, 1982.

Miller, Capt. Bill. *Tampa Triangle Dead Zone.* St. Petersburg, FL: Tickets to Adventure Inc., 1977.

"Mulberry Man Slips on Sardines, Falls into Tampa Bay." *St. Petersburg Times,* October 1, 2008.

Pittman, Craig. "Driver Goes Three Miles with Lodged Body." *St. Petersburg Times,* October 20, 2005.

CHAPTER 13: MURDER ON OCEAN DRIVE

Henneberger, Melinda. "At Play in Old Miami Beach." *New York Times,* November 13, 1994.

Lacayo, Richard. "Tagged for Murder." *Time,* July 28, 1997.

Orth, Maureen. "The Killer's Trail," *Vanity Fair,* September 1997.

———. *Vulgar Favors.* New York: Random House, 1999.

Steighorst, Tom, and Meredith Grossman. "Another Economic Black Eye?" *Sun Sentinel,* July 16, 1997.

Yanez, Luisa, and Sean Piccoli. "Remembering 'One of Us.'" *Sun Sentinel,* July 19, 1997.

CHAPTER 14: ANCIENT MYSTERY SURROUNDED BY SKYSCRAPERS

Bell, Maya. "Despite Efforts, Miami Circle's Secrets Lie Buried." *Orlando Sentinel,* January 2, 2008.

Carr, Bob. "An Ancient Legacy Is Rescued among the Skyscrapers." *Forum,* Winter 2001.

Fields, Gregg. "Circle Developer Attracts Controversy." *Miami Herald,* February 19, 1999.

Historical Museum of Southern Florida News Release. "Historical Museum Signs Sublease with State of Florida to Manage the Miami Circle." March 14, 2008.

Interview with Bob Carr, archeologist. www.hmsf.org.

Kelly, Jim. "Magic Primeval, Part 2." *Miami New Times,* November 23, 2000.

Schulman, Sandra Hale. "America's Stonehenge Surrounded by Condos and Controversy." *Indian Country News,* April 11, 2011.

Viglucci, Andres. "After 12 Years, Miami Circle Opens to the Public as a Park." *Miami Herald,* February 23, 2011.

Yanez, Luisa. "Mason Won't Budge Ancient Stone." *Sun Sentinel.* February 16, 1999.

CHAPTER 15: GOOD FOOD, PRANKS, AND GHOSTS AT THE DESERT INN

"Beware DCA's Demise." *Orlando Sentinel,* February 20, 2011.

Cortner, Marvin, ed. "Destiny Facing Huge Hurdles." *Around Osceola,* April 9, 2011.

"An Environmental Disaster." *Orlando Sentinel,* March 4, 2011.

Fletcher, Jovida. "Desert Inn Gets into Historic Register." *Orlando Sentinel,* February 16, 1994.

———. "Desert Inn Owner Tries to Uncover Restaurant's History." *Orlando Sentinel,* March 29, 1992.

Hundley, Kris. "Yeehaw's Destiny Awaits." *St. Petersburg Times,* June 4, 2006.

Resen, Warren. "Desert Inn: Going Going . . . ???" *Farmer & Rancher,* November 2006.

Wallace, Daniel. "Yeehaw Junction" (photo essay). *St. Petersburg Times,* 2006.

INDEX

ABOUT THE AUTHOR

E. Lynne Wright is the author of *More Than Petticoats: Remarkable Florida Women, It Happened in Florida, Disasters and Heroic Rescues of Florida,* and *Florida: Mapping the Sunshine State through History* (with Vincent Virga), as well as short stories, nonfiction articles, essays, and book reviews in numerous newspapers and magazines. She lives in Vero Beach, Florida.